D0206068

Simone Weil

LITERATURE AND LIFE

(Formerly Modern Literature and World Dramatists)
GENERAL EDITOR: Philip Winsor

Selected list of titles:

Complete list of titles in the series available from publisher on request.

Simone Weil

Dorothy Tuck McFarland

FREDERICK UNGAR PUBLISHING CO.
NEW YORK

Copyright © 1983 by Frederick Ungar Publishing Co., Inc.
Printed in the United States of America

Library of Congress Cataloging in Publication Data

McFarland, Dorothy Tuck, 1938-
  Simone Weil.
  (Literature and life series)
  Bibliography: p.
  Includes index.
  1. Weil, Simone, 1909-1943. 2. Philosophers—
France—Biography. I. Title. II. Series.
B2430.W474M33 1983   194   [B]   82-25609
ISBN 0-8044-2604-X

Acknowledgments

I am grateful to publishers of the following standard works for allowing me to use my own translation of brief passages:

Waiting for God, by Simone Weil, copyright 1951, G.P. Putnam's Sons; *The Need for Roots*, by Simone Weil, copyright 1952, G.P. Putnam's Sons.

The Notebooks of Simone Weil, copyright 1956, Routledge & Kegan Paul Ltd.; *Intimations of Christianity among the Ancient Greeks*, by Simone Weil, copyright 1957, Routledge & Kegan Paul Ltd.; *Oppression and Liberty*, by Simone Weil, copyright 1958, Routledge & Kegan Paul Ltd.

Selected Essays, by Simone Weil, copyright 1962, Oxford University Press; *Seventy Letters*, by Simone Weil, copyright 1965, Oxford University Press; *On Science, Necessity, and the Love of God*, by Simone Weil, copyright 1968, Oxford University Press.

La Vie de Simone Weil, by Simone Pétrement, copyright 1973, Librairie Arthème Fayard.

Lectures on Philosophy, by Simone Weil, copyright 1978, Cambridge University Press.

I would also like to thank Fr. Mark Delery, OCSO, Fr. Richard Downs, CSC, and Leone Stein, all of whom read the manuscript in various stages and offered valuable help; Wilhelmina Van Ness, who not only read and criticized the manuscript but generously shared the fruits of many years of research and thought on Simone Weil with me; Dr. André Weil and Sylvie Weil, who were generous with their time in talking to me about their family; and my husband, Gerald McFarland, who gave unstinting support to the project.

for
W. V. N.

The object of my research is not the supernatural, but this world. The supernatural is the light. One must not be so bold as to make an object of it, or else one degrades it.

—Simone Weil, 1942

Abbreviations Used in the Text

Each quotation from Simone Weil's works in the text is followed by the initial letters of the volume from which it is taken and the page reference. For the most part, references are to English translations where they exist. Occasionally I have used my own more literal translation rather than the existing English translation; in such cases I refer the reader to the passage in the French edition and follow with a reference locating it in the published English translation.

AD	*Attente de Dieu*
CO	*La Condition ouvrière*
E	*L'Enracinement*
EHP	*Écrits historiques et politiques*
EL	*Écrits de Londres*
FLN	*First and Last Notebooks*
GG	*Gravity and Grace*
GTG	*Gateway to God*
I	*The Iliad, or The Poem of Force*
IC	*Intimations of Christianity among the Ancient Greeks*
IP	*Intuitions pré-chrétiennes*
L	*Seventy Letters*

Contents

Simone Weil

Some Problems in Approaching Simone Weil

Simone Weil (1909–43) was trained as a philosopher and was by profession a teacher of philosophy. She was also a student of classical and modern history, science and literature, a political activist and theorist, a revolutionary who seriously asked why revolutions don't work, a critic of modern civilization, a combatant in the Spanish Civil War, a laborer in French fields and factories, a member of the French Resistance in London in 1943, and in the last years of her life, a mystic. She was one of the most unusual and brilliant minds of the twentieth century. Since her death from malnutrition and tuberculosis in London at the age of thirty-four, seventeen volumes of her writings have been published in France (about three-fourths of this material has been translated into English) and she has become if not exactly widely read at least rather widely known, as much for her intransigence, dedication, and uncompromising loyalty to her "impractical" ideals as for the scope and authenticity of her writings.

Weil's effect on people during her lifetime was powerful, and the typical response to her was strongly ambivalent. She was unique to the point of seeming alien—

a "painted bird," to borrow Jerzy Kosinski's phrase. The poet Jean Tortel, who met her in 1940, evokes the quality of "difference" which surrounded her, a quality at once physical and psychological, one that both attracted and repelled. He described her as a "kind of bodiless black bird folded in on itself," wearing a "vast black cape which she never took off and which flapped against her calves." Motionless, silent, she sat alone at the end of an old sofa piled high with books and magazines in the garret of the *Cahiers du Sud* in Marseilles, "alien and attentive, at once watchful and remote." Often she immersed herself in reading while all around her people engaged in conversation. She was "a presence.... Unusual and perhaps incomprehensible...a little formidable (a bit feared)." Tortel noted that when she directed her attention to someone, she had "a sort of interrogative avidity which I never encountered elsewhere." He found the intensity of her attention "almost insupportable"; sometimes he felt "a need to escape from this denuding, harrowing gaze" that seized the person subjected to it and left him "stripped," having transported him "in spite of himself into the domain of Being." Yet at the same time he found in her a suppliant, almost beseeching quality. Her mouth seemed to him "imploring"; her "large, too-moist lips" seemed ceaselessly to be making a request "at once smiling and desperate"; her smile seemed always to contain "some indescribable appeal.... some indescribable supplication."[1]

She demanded of those she came in contact with something close to the enormously high standards she set for herself. Tortel speaks of the way she rendered "untouchable" writers or texts she passionately admired by demanding that others approach them "not only with intelligence but also with an indescribable integrity."[2] Another friend, Jean Duperray, observed that it was difficult for her to tolerate "what seemed to her to be an inconsistency or a failing in her comrades" and that she "worked hard to destroy what in her opinion tarnished the character of her friends."[3] Similarly, the closer she was to a group—whether the various organizations of the left or the Catholic Church—the more pained she was by its shortcomings and self-complacency and the more insistent were her demands that it recognize its failings and purify itself. Many people evidently found her not comfortable to be around in life, and she has continued to arouse discomfort as well as admiration after her death.

Her extensive learning, her penetrating intelligence, her moral vision, and her outsider's stance combined to give Weil a unique perspective on the whole phenomenon of modern civilization. She criticized both the spiritual and social consequences of the West's adulation of science and technology and the widespread belief in the limitless possibilities of material expansion. She argued that the values which have made for the political and technological power of the West are false values—related to what she called the worship of force—and that our technological, political, and social creations, which so much surpass in magnitude the scale of the human individual, have escaped conscious control and direction and are in the process of leading us to destruction. Her analysis of the ideas of false greatness—in history, art, literature, and science—that have shaped and are continuing to shape Western civilization is one of the truly great insights into what one might call Western psychology. Unfortunately, it is an insight which is often dismissed as a curiosity or an aberration because she traces its roots—the identification of temporal power with spiritual good—to the ancient Hebrews and the Romans, and it is extremely hard for many readers, when one gets down to such particulars, to be open to what she is saying. But Europe, she argued, felt the same horror in regard to Hitler in 1940 that the Mediterranean world felt in regard to Rome around the beginning of the Christian era; and Hitler's program to exterminate the "degenerate" races to prevent contamination of Aryan purity had the same justification as the Old Testament extermination of the idolatrous Canaanites to prevent spiritual contamination of Hebrew monotheism.

She was not, of course, advocating anti-Romanism or anti-Semitism but was arguing for a clearer discrimination of what is good and what is evil in the heritage of the West, for a moral clarification of the cultural myths which work on us and out of which we enact and create history. Not to condemn the Roman conquest of the Mediterranean world, not to condemn the Old Testament massacres, was in her eyes to invite their repetition.

Weil's critical stance vis-à-vis the Old Testament* has sometimes led to the charge that she was an anti-Semitic Jew. Moreover, from a post-World War II point of view in particular, her critical attitude toward Judaism and her refusal to identify herself as a Jew have seemed to many people to be a disturbing inconsistency, given her extraordinary sympathy for others suffering affliction and given the unbelievable horrors which were being perpetrated against the Jews in Europe. However, in assessing her attitude toward Jews and Judaism, one should keep several factors in mind. First, there is the value Weil placed on universalism. The spirit of the twentieth century has, in a general way, tended toward an affirmation of ethnicity and cultural pluralism and away from the universalism based on a belief in the oneness of human reason that flourished in the seventeenth and eight-

---

*It should be noted that Weil did not reject the Old Testament in toto; some of it—the early chapters of Genesis, parts of the Psalms and the Prophets, and the Book of Job and the Song of Solomon—she praised as "beautiful and pure." (285 NR) She objected primarily to the preexilic writings, especially those which identified triumphant Hebrew nationalism with the will of God, and to the noncritical Christian acceptance of these stories as "sacred texts." (129 L)

teenth centuries. Here as in many other areas, Simone Weil affirmed the older values. Second, Weil's refusal to identify herself as a Jew should be viewed in conjunction with her own sense of personal vocation, which demanded that she not identify with any group; as she put it, she felt obliged to remain a "stranger and an exile in relation to every human circle without exception." (54 WG) Finally, her attitude toward Jewish assimilation should be seen as a product of the liberal French culture in which she was raised. Even if Hannah Arendt is right in her assertion that "assimilation as a group phenomenon really existed only among Jewish intellectuals,"[4] the ideal of Jewish assimilation, rooted in the egalitarian ideology of the French Revolution, was a living ideal in the atmosphere in which Simone Weil grew up. For more than a hundred years, French-born or naturalized Jews had been, under the law, indistinguishable from other French citizens; at least in theory, Jews were defined only in terms of their adherence to the Jewish religion, not in terms of their ethnic background. People like Weil's parents, who were nonreligious and had no ties to the Jewish community, often considered themselves completely French. Weil herself always felt that the Hebrew tradition was foreign to her and the "Christian, French, Hellenic tradition"[5] had been hers from childhood. In addition, she placed a great deal of value on the ideal of Jewish assimilation; even after the twentieth-century influx of ethnically conscious Jewish immigrants from Eastern Europe changed the attitude of many Jews and non-Jews alike in regard to both the possibility and the desirability of assimilation, Weil remained convinced that the absorption of Jews into the culture of the countries in which they lived was the only real solution to the problem of European anti-Semitism. As long as there was what she called a "crystallized Jewish minority," she believed that sooner or later it would become the object of "atrocities."[6]

Because she made relatively few references to the persecution of the Jews,* Weil has also been criticized for caring more about victims of oppression remote from her in space or time than she did about "people with her family name."[7] Her position, however, was that injustice must be condemned universally; when she speaks of the persecution of the Jews, she always, at the same time, mentions other peoples (the Indochinese especially, who at that time were under French colonial rule) who have been treated with terrible cruelty and on whose behalf little public outcry has been made. She goes so far as to suggest that if injustice is not universally condemned, it will not be condemned at all. Speaking of the French who were collaborating with the Germans during the Occupation, she writes with dry and deadly irony, "The cruelties accompanying the German system ought, it is true, to have stopped them. But they may either not have heard anything about them, or supposed them to have been invented by a lying propaganda, or regarded them as of little importance, because the victims were people of inferior category. Is it not just as easy to be ignorant of the cruelties of the Germans towards the Jews or the Czechs as it is of those of the French toward the Annamites?" (145 NR)

Weil was not only a critic of accepted ways of thinking; she was also a builder. From her early writings until the end of her life she was preoccupied with the problem of conceiving a nonoppressive form of civilization, one which fostered individual thought, initiative, and responsibility and one in which labor would not be despised but would be accorded a position of value and dignity.

---

*It should be remembered that Weil died in 1943, before anything like the full extent and the full horror of the Holocaust was known.

The remedy she envisaged at the end of her life for the uprooted condition of modern Europe involved both a re-rooting of Europe in the neglected spiritual dimensions of the culture of ancient Greece and a transformed conception of manual labor. The very reason that the ancient Greeks despised labor—its intimate connection with the physical necessities of the human condition[x]—became for Weil the source of its spiritual value. She sketched what might be called a theology of labor in which physical labor is understood as an image of the obedience of matter to necessity, to the divine order of the universe, which she saw as a reflection of the very thought, the Wisdom, of God.

Contrary to what has been frequently said, Weil's thought is not fragmentary. Quite the opposite; it is so much all of a piece that with very few exceptions it is almost impossible to appreciate the full dimensions of any one part read singly and out of relationship to the whole. Unfortunately, her work has been edited and published, especially in English, largely in a fragmentary and unchronological way. Because of this, she has been often regarded primarily as a brilliant aphorist, and the sustained and developing relationships that characterize her thinking have gone unrecognized. The relative neglect of her thought, in comparison to the interest in her life, may be partly due to these difficulties. In addition, there is a translation problem. A close translation of Weil's precise and lucid French is sometimes rather stilted in English, and a freer translation tends to lose both the metaphoric power of the original and Weil's distinctive voice. There is also what one might call a second-level translation problem that has to do with the carrying across of ideas from one form of cultural expression to another and, ultimately, from the matrix of one mind to another. I have tried to facilitate this second level of translation by tracing the development and the complex interrelationship of the major ideas in Weil's writing and by sketching the relation of her thought to her life and to the world in which she lived.

Because the image of Weil that has been projected by most newspaper and magazine reviews has a definite tendency to be exaggerated and distorted, to emphasize what is different, extreme, angular, unsympathetic, even "inhuman" about her, I have tried to present a demythologized picture of her, one that recognizes and respects the complexity of her character and does not reject aspects of it that seem alien to the modern temper. She was an independent thinker of genius, and her very independence—her insistence on questioning orthodoxies, her refusal to accept anything simply because it was the reigning opinion of whatever authorities—has placed her outside of much mainstream thinking. It is possible that there has been so much emphasis on what is extreme or absurd in Weil's life because of the challenge she presents to different aspects of mainstream thinking; an approach that on the one hand praises her intellectual gifts and achievements and on the other constructs a grotesque portrait of the woman herself may be an attempt to avoid confronting seriously what she has to say.

Weil's perspective is not, and should not be considered to be, the only possible perspective on the problems she addresses; but a mind like hers appears once in a century, if that often, and her thought has a depth of penetration and breadth of scope that are, at times, nothing less than awesome. Her late thought is also characterized by a complex, almost dialectical structure that must be taken into consideration if she is to be adequately understood. Typically, she approaches a problem both from the vantage point of human experience in the world and from the point of view of eternity, and then explores the contradictions that result. Indeed, in her late writing Weil explicitly sees contradictions as a lever which can be used to raise her (and our) understanding of a given problem to a higher and more complex level, thereby enlarging and deepening the "composition on many planes" which constitutes one's perception of reality. She is thus, in a sense, more of a relativist than a casual reading of her works might suggest, although hers is an unusual kind of relativism, anchored in a belief in the existence of absolute truth and in the human need to make representations of that truth—representations, however, that are always in need of correction. For all her belief in, and orientation toward, absolute truth, her method of thinking is altogether at odds with the kind of thinking that accepts or supports orthodoxies, and this accounts at least in part for her difficulties with the orthodoxies of the political left and, later, the Catholic Church. Both Weil herself and her writings embody a paradoxical tension between absolute certainty and a radical openness that is almost a kind of agnosticism; she spoke and wrote with unyielding conviction (she was said never to give way in an argument), but at the same time she was fully aware of the inadequacy of her conceptions to embrace what was by definition beyond her. "I am absolutely certain," she wrote in her Marseilles *Notebooks* (1940–42), "that there is a God, in the sense that I am absolutely certain that my love is not illusory. I am absolutely certain that there is not a God, in the sense that I am absolutely certain that there is nothing real which bears a resemblance to what I am able to conceive when I pronounce that name, since I am unable to conceive God—But that thing, which I am unable to conceive, is not an illusion. . . ." (127 N)

Not only Simone Weil's methods of thought but many of her ideas themselves seem very foreign to the secularized, positivistic, progressive thought that has dominated our era. For instance, she wrote, when she was about twenty-four, "I believe in the value of suffering, so long as one makes every [legitimate] effort to escape it." (3 FLN) That there can be any value at all in suffering is not an idea that has much currency in the latter half of the twentieth century, which is one of the reasons her lived witness to its value is of such importance. The problems that such unconventional ideas present to the reader provide in themselves an exercise in learning how to think on another level. As one perceptive critic wrote, "Weil herself . . . is a subject that familiarizes one with a quality of assertion that is vastly different from *liking* and *disliking*. She lives in that rarefied place where opinions and arguments are not relevant, where the issues are those of acceptance and non-acceptance. It is a dangerous land to inhabit permanently, but an occasional point of view that is taken from it may be the liberating equivalent of an extended vacation from the Cave."[9]

Understanding Simone Weil demands both openness to difficult and sometimes disturbing ideas and a serious effort of attention. Without such attention, Weil believed, the transmission of truth between human beings was not possible. In one of her last works, she wrote:

A truth never appears except in the mind of a particular human being. How will he communicate it? If he tries to expound it, no one will listen to him, for other people, not being familiar with this truth, won't recognize it for what it is; they will not know that what he is saying is true; they will not pay enough attention to it to become aware of it, for they will have no reason to make the necessary effort of attention.

But friendship, admiration, sympathy, or any other favorable sort of feeling would naturally dispose them to pay a certain degree of attention. A man who has something new to say—for no attention is necessary when it is a matter of platitudes—can only be listened to at first by those who love him. (262 E; cf. 207 NR)

1

1909–1930

Simone Weil was born in Paris on Feburary 3, 1909, the second child of a well-to-do, highly cultured professional family. Her parents, Dr. Bernard Weil and Selma Reinherz Weil (the family pronounces the name "Vey"), were naturalized French citizens who had been born, respectively, in Strasbourg and Rostov-on-Don. The family was of Jewish descent on both sides, but the Weils maintained no Jewish identity and considered themselves French. The children were never told by their parents that they were Jewish, and Simone apparently did not learn that her family heritage was Jewish until she was about ten years old.[1]

The family was extremely close, and the influence of Mme Weil in particular was strong. Mme Weil was a passionate, possessive woman in whom great and unyielding strength was masked by a wonderful softness of manner. Affectionate and generous, she was able "to persuade one with so much ardor and so pleasantly that one felt overwhelmed. Her authority was felt despite a real desire on her part to be effacing. She imposed herself naturally because of her courage (her daring, even), her acumen, her passionate love of her dear ones...."[2] Something of her almost overwhelming protectiveness is suggested in the account of Simone's childhood which she gave to Simone's friend and biographer Simone Pétrement, as well as in the solicitous concern she showed for her daughter throughout her life.

According to Mme Weil's recollection of her daughter's childhood, Simone was sickly; Mme Weil emphasized Simone's early eating problems in babyhood, stressed the seriousness of the appendectomy the child underwent at age three, and felt that Simone was slow to recover from the usual childhood illnesses. She was chronically concerned about both children—but Simone in particular—exhausting themselves. Probably because of Dr. Weil's profession—he was a physician—and Mme Weil's interest in medicine (she had wanted, as a young girl, to be a doctor), the whole family was extremely conscious of germs and almost comically scrupulous about antisepsis.[3] But as far as actual illness was concerned, Simone does not seem to have suffered more than anyone else in the family[4]; during her childhood, her brother André and her mother both had appendicitis, her father had bouts of serious illness, and her mother frequently went to watering places in hopes of improving her health.

Mme Weil's resolute and protective character is apparent in the way she shepherded the family and kept it together during World War I. When the war broke out in 1914, Dr. Weil volunteered and was posted to a hospital in Neufchâteau, halfway across France toward Strasbourg. Mme Weil had no intention of allowing the family to be separated from him. Disregarding military orders, she gathered her mother and the children and followed him, taking lodgings in the town.[5] After six months in Neufchâteau Dr. Weil was sent to Menton, on the Mediterranean, to recuperate from an illness; the family— now with official permission—again followed him. In

April 1915 he was assigned to Mayenne, about halfway between Paris and the Atlantic coast; the family settled there for a year and a half until the doctor was transferred to Algeria. Apparently it was quite impossible for Mme Weil to get the family to Algeria, and she, her mother, and the children returned for a few months to Paris. In the beginning of 1916 the doctor was assigned to Chartres; the family rejoined him there for another year and a half, until he was transferred to Laval, not far from Mayenne, in September 1917. They remained at Laval until he was demobilized in January 1919.

Although Simone Weil made only a few comments about it in later life, it would seem that the war affected her very deeply; it was probably the primary external cause of her obsession with suffering and affliction. As a child she was both in close proximity to the war and protected from it, and all her life she seemed to want to break through the protective barriers that separated her, as a noncombatant, from the suffering experienced by those directly involved in war. She was close enough to the war, as a child, to actually see its consequences in human suffering. "The hospitals are packed to overflowing with sick and wounded," Mme Weil wrote when they were in Neufchâteau. "We go almost every day to the hospitals to bring the patients oranges, crackers, and newspapers.... one is ashamed to do so little when faced by such boundless misery!"[6]

The self-sacrificial climate fostered by the war aroused a fervent response in Simone. Sacrifice and a certain practical asceticism were asked of everyone, and Simone and André were encouraged by their mother to forgo sugar and chocolate and to save up their ration to send to their *filleuls de guerre* ("war godsons")—soldiers whose families were behind the front lines, who could not receive packages from home, and who were "adopted" by other French families. Simone not only saved her sugar but did chores to earn money with which to buy modest, useful gifts—socks, a flashlight—to send to her "godson."[7]

Simone's childhood capacity for self-denial has been exaggerated in some biographical accounts to the extent that it seems either part of a saint's legend or evidence of neurosis; it should be remembered that André and many other French children were also giving up their sugar and chocolate and that under the circumstances of war, an idealization of heroism and self-sacrifice is not unnatural. Moreover, Simone's capacity for compassion and sacrifice was not unbalanced; she was, indeed, capable of great generosity, but she was also a strong-willed, spirited, mischievous, sensitive, and affectionate child.

After the end of the war, the Weils settled down again in their apartment on the Boulevard Saint-Michel, not far from the Luxembourg gardens.[8] Mme Weil saw to it that her children received the best education possible. During the war years, when they had moved frequently, the children attended lycées only intermittently and for the most part had private tutors, a circumstance which greatly facilitated their intellectual development. Mme Weil had been very pleased with André's prewar lycée teacher, who had taught him to think and not simply to memorize, and she took pains to see that Simone's first tutors taught her to use her mind and not just to work mechanically.[9] Both children were, quite literally, geniuses, and their intellectual precocity is apparent in some of the ways they devised to amuse themselves. They memorized long passages from the classic works of French drama (*Cyrano de Bergerac* was Simone's favorite when she was six) and declaimed them to each other with great dramatic emphasis, and they invented complicated word games which the cousins with whom they sometimes played were quite unable to follow. But they were also encouraged to develop in nonintellectual areas: they had music, gymnastic, dancing, and swimming lessons. They loved nature, and the family always spent summer vacations at the beach, in the country, or in the mountains. If, as sometimes happened, André took his Greek grammar with him when he went fishing or Simone was late for lunch because she was reading *Crime and Punishment* on the dunes and forgot about the time,[10] they were not always immersed in books. They played soccer together, did gymnastics on the beach, took long bicycle rides and walks with their parents, and on occasion went on two-week family walking tours.[11]

Although Simone Weil had a great love of music in adult life, she did not continue for very long the piano lessons she began at the age of seven, possibly because she was not adept manually. She also had great difficulty, at the outset, with handwriting and drawing in school. (However, in late adolescence she began to discipline her formless writing into what would become a clear, fluid, unadornedly simple but distinctive and lovely hand; she may be illustrative of the Zen saying that the best calligrapher is not the one who has great native facility but the one who has encountered much difficulty in learning.) Critics have sometimes—unfairly, I believe—used her manual awkwardness and moral seriousness to cast her as a comic figure. While Simone Weil's poor coordination was undoubtedly a handicap to her in some degree, she disciplined herself through sports, some of which she learned passably well and seemed to enjoy a great deal (in adulthood she was an avid hiker, and she swam and skied), and in the factory and in her periods as a farm laborer she made heroic efforts to perform competently the tasks assigned her and for the most part managed to do so. Her inability to do physical things unconsciously and easily probably made it necessary for her to learn physical disciplines through a conscious analysis of the movements involved, and this in turn may be related to her interest, as a young philosopher, in understanding the role of bodily movement in perception and concept formation.

Early adolescence was, by Simone Weil's own later account, a time of "bottomless despair" for her because she believed that her intellectual abilities were "mediocre." This judgment was based partly on her comparison of herself with André, who was extremely gifted in mathematics and whose youthful precocity she compared to Pascal's. André was also three years older than she, and his greater intellectual maturity must have increased her feeling that her own abilities were inadequate. Moreover, during much of this time (1921–23) she was suffering under a critical and disparaging schoolmistress whose belittling remarks she took very seriously.

Weil's aspirations were extremely high; according to her later account, even at the age of fourteen she aspired to nothing less than the "realm of truth," which she believed was accessible only to genius. "I did not mind having no visible success," she wrote in 1942, describing this adolescent crisis, "but what did grieve me was the idea of being excluded from that transcendent kingdom to which only the truly great have access and wherein truth abides." (64 WG) Finally, "after months of inward darkness," she suddenly received the conviction that "any human being...can penetrate to the kingdom of truth reserved for genius, if only he longs for truth and perpetually concentrates all his attention upon its attainment."

This description of the efficacy of desire alone in the spiritual realm was written late in her life, and one may question whether such a conception could be at all accurately attributed to her at fourteen. Nevertheless, in some of her earliest (and still unpublished) writing there are astonishing prefigurations of her late thought. Her essay *Le beau et le bien*, written when Weil had just turned seventeen, displays an explicit concern with a

Platonic abstraction she calls the human spirit, with the unity of the beautiful and the good in an ideal or meta-physical realm, and with redemptive action which pro-ceeds from thought attentively grounded in that realm. It is clear that by early adulthood, well before the be-ginning of her mystical experiences in 1937–38, she was fully and consciously dedicated to the "Search for the Good." (219 LP) In 1934, when she was twenty-five, Weil spoke of attention as a method of illumination (92 LP), was oriented toward the contemplation of the "un-changing patterns of things," (220 LP) and emphasized the value of moral effort over intellectual gifts in the search for truth: "If anyone is not able to understand the unchanging patterns of things, that is not due to a lack of intelligence, it is due to a lack of moral stamina." (220 LP) Thus, the ambition which she articulated in 1937, just after her first mystical experience—"to raise oneself, in this life, to the level of eternal things" (87 L)—was evidently of long standing; it had been given explicit expression by the time she was twenty-five, is strongly suggested in her late adolescent writings, and in all like-lihood was formed in her even earlier.

Simone Weil's interest in manual labor and in work-ing-class people also apparently goes back to childhood. Since what evidence there is of that interest is indirect, a brief look at another life, that of a young Englishwoman named Sally Trench, may provide a helpful analogy. Beginning in the mid-1960s, Sally Trench spent a number of years caring for and living among tramps and derelicts in London. She said in an interview[12] that as a child she had thought of hoboes and tramps as romantic figures embodying a life of complete freedom; their symbolic significance drew her to them and sustained the tremen-dous compassion which enabled her to share the appall-ingly inhuman conditions in which they actually lived. Somewhat similarly, the young Simone Weil saw some-thing in workers that made her love them. Riding on the subway with Simone Pétrement when she was about sixteen, she indicated some workers and remarked that it was not only "out of a spirit of justice" that she loved them. "I love them naturally," she said. "I find them more beautiful than the bourgeois."[13] (Even today one encounters in Paris elderly workingmen whose gentleness and courtesy is unforgettably beautiful.)

Whereas for Sally Trench tramps represented a life of freedom—"nobody telling you what to do"—for Simone Weil the workers were associated with "real life." In childhood "real life" meant to her a joyful encounter with the harsh realities of matter—an encounter from which she did not want to be protected. One recalls the often-repeated anecdote about her objecting, during one of the family's numerous wartime changes of residence, to being given a lighter bundle to carry than her brother's, and refusing to move until she was given something heavier.[14] And ever since she was a child, she wrote in 1935, she had felt that a working-place—a factory—was a "place where one makes a hard and painful, but nevertheless joyful, contact with real life." (20 L) In adulthood "real life" meant to her not only the direct encounter of the mind with the necessities of the physical world, but also the mind's triumph over the forces that wear down the body and spirit; during the time she worked in Paris factories in 1934–35 she wrote, "I feel I have escaped from a world of abstractions, to find myself among real men—some good and some bad, but with a real goodness or badness. Goodness especially, when it exists in a factory, is something real; because the least act of kindness, from a mere smile to some little service, calls for a victory over fatigue and the obsession with pay...." (11–12 L)

In all likelihood Simone Weil's interest in politics and social reform was a consequence of her interest in working-class people. She was almost nine years old at the time of the Russian Revolution, perhaps old enough to understand that a tremendous social upheaval on behalf of the dignity of working people had taken place. By the age of eleven she was aligning herself with the workers and was aware of the need to change existing economic conditions: missing from the house one day, she was found on the Boulevard Saint-Michel attending a demonstration held by the unemployed.[15] Whatever its origin, Weil's interest in politics had its roots in her own personal response to the world and was not implanted in her by her parents or teachers. Her parents had no political passions, and politics was not discussed at home.[16] Nevertheless, by her mid-teens she was showing a consuming interest in politics; she bought newspapers every day— "preferably extremist ones," her biographer Simone Pétrement reports—and she was often seen at the Lycée Victor-Duruy carrying a copy of the communist newspaper *L'Humanité*. "Everything to do with social agitation," Pétrement writes of this period, "interested her passionately."[17]

Simone Weil had passed her first baccalaureat examination* in June 1924, when she was fifteen years old. The following autumn she enrolled in the Lycée Victor-Duruy in order to study philosophy under the eminent philosopher René le Senne, and she received her baccalaureat in philosophy in June 1925. She had decided on her future profession—she would be a teacher of philosophy—and in the fall of 1925 she entered the Lycée Henri IV to embark on the two- to three-year course of study necessary to prepare for the examinations required for entrance into the École Normale Supérieure, the *grande école* in which the elite of upper lycée and university teachers are trained. Her choice of the Lycée Henri IV

---

*Baccalaureat examinations are usually taken at the age of 17 or 18. The possession of the baccalaureat certificate enables one to enter the university; to enter one of the *grandes écoles* it is necessary to pass further qualifying examinations.

for her École Normale preparation also enabled her to
study philosophy under the renowned Alain (Émile Char-
tier), an enormously popular teacher and prolific essayist
who was a formative influence on a whole generation of
French intellectuals.

Simone Pétrement—who met Simone Weil when
both were Alain's students—believes that Weil's philosophy "began to take shape" in Alain's class and that
she owed to him "an essential part of her thought"[18];
however, she qualifies this statement by observing that
many of the ideas that Simone Weil had in common with
Alain had already been formed in her before she became
his student: "The revolt against the social order, the feelings of indignation toward the powers-that-be, the choice
of the poor as comrades and companions—all this,"
Pétrement writes, "had not come from Alain."[19]

Alain's teaching drew heavily on Plato, Descartes,
Spinoza, Kant, Maine de Biran, Jules Lachelier, and his
own teacher, Jules Lagneau. Broadly speaking, all these
men can be said to belong to the tradition which the
French call "philosophies of reflection," that is, philosophies in which the individual mind, through the act of
thought, recognizes its intimate relationship to Being, to
Thought itself. Historically, the orientation of philosophy
toward the realm of Being has often tended to have as
its counterpart a turning away from and a devaluation of
the world of things, and such philosophies have tended
to produce a dualism of mind/body, thought/action, es-
sence/existence in which body, action, and existence are
relegated to an inferior role. The specifically French line
of reflective philosophy which begins with Maine de Biran
in the early nineteenth century attempted to bridge the
mind/body split by positing that knowledge of the thinking consciousness, of the self, is not dependent on the
activity of the mind alone but on the mind's relation to
the body, on willed bodily movement, and hence on
action in the world.

Jules Lagneau, following Maine de Biran, taught that the self "knows itself only in the action which it exercises on the exterior world." In this concept of the dependence of self-knowledge on action in the world he found "a great truth, which is that the individual soul and the universe are not able to be conceived separately, and also that it is action which makes known the unity of the two and at the same time the opposition of the two."[20] Alain, who had been taught by Lagneau, made the reality of the act of reflective thought—which for him was to will the good, or simply to will—dependent not on the activity of the mind alone but on the incarnation of thought in action. As Pétrement summarizes it, he taught that the "will does not exist except in action."[21]

Simone Weil, from the time of her first published writing (1929) until the end of the life, was concerned with the relationship between thought and action in the world. Basically, she follows Lagneau and Alain in seeing action in the world as a means of knowledge of the thinking self and hence of the world of value; even in her later writings, which are more purely Platonic and which emphasize the necessity of directing one's attention to the good that is outside this world, Weil continues to try to relate the world of value to the material world. For her, thought that turns away from the world does so in order to contemplate its relationship to the world of value so that the mind illuminated by value can then bring that illumination into the world. As she wrote in a late unpublished text, detached thought "has as its object a way of living, a better life, not elsewhere but in this world and immediately."[22]

While at the Lycée Henri IV (1925–28) Simone Weil became friends with a student named Pierre Letellier. At that time, Pétrement reports, Simone Weil believed that the "most accomplished and the most human man was the man who was both a manual worker and a

thinker."[23] Pierre Letellier's father, Leon Letellier, embodied for her that human ideal. The son of a Norman
peasant family, he had run away to sea at sixteen and
worked as a seaman until well into adulthood; then he
returned to school and, about the age of thirty, studied
under Jules Lagneau. Letellier published his notes of
Lagneau's lectures, and after Letellier's death in 1926,
a collection of extracts from his own writings was published.

In this early stage of Simone Weil's interest in the
worker figure—she was eighteen—she was not yet
thinking of work, as she would later, as a way of fusing
thought and action but as a means of training in moral
courage. In a brief essay she wrote on Letellier she views
his work experience as a strengthening of the spirit that
prepared him for his intellectual odyssey:

Having learned, on the Newfoundland boats, what human beings
are capable of by overcoming apparently insurmountable fatigue and suffering every day, he could hardly allow himself
to be seduced by brilliant arguments which demonstrate that
man is not free, that there is no human spirit or that truth is
only a word; he remained as vigorously deaf to academic eloquence as he had remained deaf, on the ocean, to the much
more moving eloquence of his own exhausted body; and he
recognized in skepticism not error but cowardice. . . . He never
allowed himself to yield to the modern followers of Callicles
who adore only power and prove that the love of men is a
virtue of the weak. . . . In him, as doubtless in all truly strong
men, strength found its perfection in love.[24]

In order to fully understand the physical reality of
work as well as its moral and philosophical implications,
Weil felt it necessary to do manual labor herself. While
visiting the Letellier family farm in Normandy in the
summer of 1927 she worked in the fields. She applied
for civilian service work in Lichtenstein[25] in the summer
of 1928 but was turned down because she specified labor
in the fields (women were appointed to kitchen tasks).

In the summer of 1929 she went to visit relatives in the Jura region and managed to escape family surveillance enough to spend some ten-hour days working in the potato fields.[26] In the summer of 1931, vacationing with her parents in the seaside village of Reville (near Cherbourg), she inquired among the fishermen until she found a crew willing to allow her to go out in their boat and work with them.[27]

Weil's own experience as a manual laborer undoubtedly contributed to her analysis of the way the human mind comes to know the material world. She began to try to analyze the part work plays in knowledge of the world in her first two published essays, *De la perception ou l'aventure de Protée* and *Du temps*, which appeared in Alain's magazine *Libres Propos* in May and August 1929. The first essay is an exploration of the process by which sense impressions, which are passively received, which give us pleasure or pain but "teach us nothing about the world," are transformed into signs pointing, as it were, to the idea of space. Sense impressions are like the shape-changing Proteus of Greek mythology; according to the myth, only when Menelaus had firmly held on to Proteus throughout all his transformations did the latter assume his true form. Analogously, Weil writes, when one has grasped the idea of space, sense impressions are constrained to tell the truth, to become a means of knowing the world. The grasp of space comes about through work, for the "law of exterior relationship which defines space"—that is, the impossibility of passing "from one point to another without passing through all the intermediate points"—is the same as the "law of work," the law that governs action in the world. One cannot act—make one's will effective in the world—without passing through all the intermediate steps (both in space and in time) that separate the condition in which one is from the condition in which one would like to be.

Work not only mediates the knowledge of extension

(in Cartesian terms, extension is the fundamental characteristic of matter), it brings forcefully and inescapably
the knowledge of the reality of the external world. As
Weil would say to her philosophy students a few years
later, the "question of the reality of the external world
[is] quite a simple one: the simple fact that taking 100
paces is something different from saying '100 paces' is
proof of its reality." (75 LDP; cf. 72 LP) Work also
defines the human condition in relation to the world. The
worker knows that he is not all-powerful, since he cannot
achieve his desires directly, simply by willing; but he
also knows that he is not totally without power in relation
to the world, for through the proper use of both his mind
and his body he can act on the world and change it, albeit
only partially. The world infinitely surpasses him in magnitude, power, and complexity; nevertheless, to the degree that he understands the ideas of space, time, and
causality, all of which are mediated through work, he is
not overwhelmed by this tremendous power but is able
to use it. Weil offered (in a slightly later essay on the
same topic) a striking image to illustrate this idea: "though
astronomy does not give us any real power over the sky,
still it makes the sky enter into our realm, to the point
that the pilot dares to use these stars—which the power
of all humanity together could not cause to deviate from
their course by a hairsbreadth—as his instruments." (94
SS)

Simone Weil elaborated her ideas on work and perception in her diploma dissertation for the École Normale,
written during the 1929–30 school year. The dissertation
also attempts to demonstrate that modern science, in rejecting the commonsense thinking of ordinary human
beings as an inadequate instrument of knowledge, is not
in accord with the thought of Descartes, whom Weil
regarded as its founder. Called *Science et perception dans
Descartes*, the dissertation begins by asking whether there
is a method for obtaining truth which can be employed

by all human beings or whether truth belongs to a realm
to which only an elite has entry. "Nothing is more difficult," she writes, "and at the same time nothing is more
important for each man to know. For it is nothing less
than a question of knowing whether I ought to submit
the conduct of my life to the authority of scientific thinkers, or solely to the light of my own reason; or
rather...whether science will bring me liberty, or legitimate chains." (13 SS)

Weil argues that the first method of discovering in-
controvertible truths was that of the Greek Thales, whom
she regarded as the inventor of geometry. Weil celebrated
the advent of Thales as "the greatest moment in history,"
for until then all knowledge had been uncertain, a matter
of "trials and conjectures"; but "from the moment that
Thales...invented geometry, it [humanity] knew." (12
SS) Although Thales was "not limited by common
thought," nevertheless his geometry was based on it; his
fundamental theorem on the relationship between similar
triangles starts from objects in the world—a man, a pyr-
amid, and the lengths of their shadows—and is based
on ordinary perception of those objects. Such a beginning
would seem logically, Weil goes on, to promise a science
in which the exercise of human reason would have as its
material the sensible world. However, both the later
Greeks and modern scientists, finding Thales's thought
too earthbound, moved further and further toward pure
abstraction. Reasoning not only became increasingly detached from the world but was made the prerogative of
specialists. Such a situation was not, Weil suspected, in
accord with the true nature of science. Pointing out some
contradictions in modern science, she wondered whether
such contradictions were a sign "that scientists, in separating as they do scientific thought from common thought,
are guided by their own prejudices rather than by the
nature of science." To answer this question she went back
to the origin of modern science, to the "double revolution

by which physics became an application of mathematics and geometry became algebra: in other words, to Descartes." (17 SS)

Despite his prominent position in the development of modern philosophic idealism, despite the abstractness of his analytic geometry, Descartes actually combined, Simone Weil argues in the first part of her dissertation, an extreme idealism with an extreme realism. Although he refused to accept, in his search for indubitable knowledge, the testimony of the senses because they could be misleading, he did not deny the reality of the sensible world. Cartesian geometry is more abstract than classical geometry, but it is "never separated from the imagination," (40 SS) that is, from figures or images formed in the mind but based on objects in the sensible world. Cartesian science does not reject figures, "since Descartes says expressly that by them alone the ideas of all things can be fashioned." (41 SS) Nor does Cartesian science imply a separation between scientific thought and ordinary human thought: Descartes "regards every mind, as soon as it applies itself to think *comme il faut*,* as equal to the greatest genius." (44 SS) For Descartes, true philosophy was to the mind "what the eyes are to the body," a way of grasping the world; he found "common wisdom much nearer to this true philosophy . . . than are the thoughts produced by study." He regarded perception itself as being "of the same nature as science"; he found a " 'natural geometry' " in perception, " 'an action of thought' " that involves " 'reasoning similar to that which surveyors

---

*This idiom, which is usually used to describe social behavior, means "properly" or "in a well-bred way." Its literal meaning— "as it is necessary"—suggests that the behavior it describes is commendable because it is appropriate to the true (gentlemanly nature of the subject; it is "the right way to do things." Descartes uses the phrase to mean "the right way to think," the kind of thinking that is in accord with the true nature of thought.

make, when, by means of two different stations, they measure inaccessible places.'" (45–46 SS)

There is thus in Cartesian science, Weil goes on, the basis for a science quite different from the science which has actually developed from it. She then turns to Descartes's famous method of systematic doubt to determine whether the philosophy derived from it could be in accord with what she sees in his science. She does this by replicating the Cartesian method in herself, doubting all thoughts which could be in any way said to be the result of sense impressions—all thoughts of which she is the passive recipient rather than the active and sole originator.

Having separated herself from the world and from the possible deceptions of sense impressions in order to discover what she can know by pure understanding, Weil then turns to the imagination, the point of connection with the world, the "bond of action and reaction between the world and my thought," (71 SS) in order to find out how it can instruct her about the world. She finds first that the imagination has a double nature; insofar as it contains clear and simple ideas, such as number, which exist "only by an act of my attention" and therefore do not represent "an encroachment of the world on me," the imagination provides her with a means of grasping the world; but there is also an undisciplined imagination that makes her see in sensations "the most fantastic things." How, she askes herself, to connect the "docile" imagination guided by the mind with this other imagination at the mercy of sense impressions and the passions? They are rejoined, she decides, by the intermediary of work. By perception and work, sensations and emotions are no longer taken as "signs of fantastic existences" (85 SS) but as signs of the extended world which is the object of work. Thus, she concludes, "Perception is geometry in some way taking possession of the passions themselves, by means of work." (85 SS) In perception joined with work one masters the disorderly imagination, and one can begin to take possession of—know—the world.

Her choice of vocabulary—she repeatedly uses "to seize, to grasp" as synonyms of "to know"—emphasizes that knowledge of the world is a physical as well as a mental act, that it involves deliberate bodily action—work—in the world. All wisdom, Weil concludes, is implicitly contained in this embodied grasp of the mind on the world through work: "The pilot who in the tempest directs the tiller, the peasant who swings his scythe, knows himself and knows the world in the way expressed by the saying 'I think, therefore I am' and the whole cortege of ideas that goes with it." (95 SS)

Knows himself and knows the world. In this notion that knowledge of the world (science) is not separate from Socratic or reflective self-knowledge (knowledge of the realm of value) is a view of man and his relation to the world in which there is no antagonism between science and metaphysics, and Weil traces this view to the very Descartes who is usually considered responsible for the unbridgeable gulf between them. She is in this early essay plainly arguing for a reconsideration of the dominant trends in both modern science and philosophy, a reconsideration which can provide a basis for a holistic view of man and his relation both to the material world and the realm of value. She is specifically arguing for an end to the tyranny of savants and specialists of all kinds; more broadly, she is looking for a philosophical base that will not support any form of authoritarianism, and a philosophy of reflection that emphasizes the individual thinker as knower and recognizes the capacity of every individual to think *comme il faut* can provide a solid foundation for an egalitarian system. Finally, in joining the ideal form of work (methodical thought* applied to action in the

*That is, thought which has separated itself from the passions and which perceives necessity. See *Lectures on Philosophy*, p. 88.

world) with the tradition of reflective philosophy, she is arguing that every type of thinking that is truly *comme il faut* necessarily involves an overcoming of the passions, a subordination of immediate gratifications to reflective thought, and therefore opens the way to the practice of value-oriented life.

2

1931–1933

Simone Weil's philosophy gave rise naturally to her political and social theory. As she saw thoughtful and careful manual work as an essential element in the way the human being comes to know both himself and the world, she saw skilled craftsmen as the natural leaders of the working class and the potential builders of a "rational society." (23 OL) Her conception of a just society made her, initially, a revolutionary, convinced of the necessity for total change; but she was a revolutionary who did not belong to any established group and who was often highly critical of, and therefore also criticized by, the various revolutionary orthodoxies. However, for a period of several years (roughly between 1927 and 1932) she was open to the possibility that the communists might be right in their contention that it was the party and the party alone that could lead the proletariat to its triumph. Nevertheless, her own inclination led her not to the party nor to any group based primarily on a political ideology; the place to prepare the workers for their role in the new society was, she believed, in the workers' own organization, the trade unions (*syndicats*).[1]

In 1931 Simone Weil passed her *agrégation** examination and applied for a teaching position in a port or industrial city. The world was two years into an economic crisis that was steadily worsening. Unemployment was increasing, and it appeared to many that they were witnessing the collapse of capitalism predicted by Marx and that a triumphant proletarian revolution was imminent. Simone Weil, in 1931, shared these feelings; she felt that the time had come "to organize the struggle immediately" and to do what needed to be done to strengthen the working class for the task that awaited it. "The regime can continue to exist in the state of decomposition which it has reached," she wrote in November 1931, "only if lack of unity and organization and the absence of clear ideas keep the working class in its present state of weakness."[2]

In requesting a post in an industrial city, Weil hoped to be sent to a place with a large working-class population where she would be able, in addition to her professional responsibilities as a teacher, to do something to remedy the weakness of the working class. However, she had already acquired a reputation at the École Normale as a revolutionary if not a communist; she was independent, outspoken, and difficult to intimidate, and she had made at least one enemy among the administration—Célestin Bouglé, the assistant director, whom she had once challenged in class and who responded to her impertinence by referring mockingly to her as the "Red Virgin."[3] Bouglé evidently saw to it that she was sent as far away as possible, and to a place with few opportunities for revolutionary activity. She was posted to Le Puy, a small

---

*The *agrégation* is a very difficult examination taken by students leaving the École Normale. Those who pass are thereafter known as *agrégés*, addressed as "professor," and paid an additional sum (*prime d'agrégation*) above the regular teacher's salary.

city in southeastern France, some thirteen hours by train from Paris.

Le Puy, however, was only three hours by train from the industrial city of St.–Étienne. Having acquired, before she left Paris, the names of some of the revolutionary syndicalist* militants in St.-Étienne, Weil made herself known to them and for several months made the lengthy trip between Le Puy and St.-Étienne at least once a week to meet with trade union leaders and workers. Her major concern at this point was trade union unity, which was severely undermined by political differences and different conceptions of the place of politics in the trade union

*French syndicalism, which emerged in the latter half of the nineteenth century, was a nonpolitical labor movement that hoped to effect social transformation by the exercise of economic pressure in the form of the general strike, a "peaceful but relentless folding of arms that would starve out the capitalists."[4] Syndicalists often joined forces with other leftist movements. The many similarities between syndicalism and the anarchism of Proudhon and Bakunin—their common emphasis on worker self-management, their high regard for the value of work, and their view of workers as the "value-creating element in society"[5]—led to a cross-fertilization between the two groups; the *syndicats* were influenced by anarchist ideas, and the anarchists often took part in *syndicat* actions.[6] Similarly, some syndicalists became communists, especially at the time of the Russian Revolution. The revolutionary syndicalists were a dissident communist group whose leaders had been expelled from or left the party after the early promise of worker democracy in Russia gave way to government by bureacracy. (See Albertine Thévenon's introduction to Weil's *La Condition ouvrière*, p. 8.) In the revolutionary syndicalist movement Weil found support for a number of ideas—worker democracy, worker education—that were of fundamental importance to her. It is also likely that the revolutionary syndicalists' dissident communist position helped her perceive the role of the bureaucracy in Russia and its implications in terms of what might be expected from revolutions.

movement. The original federation of trade unions, the CGT (*Confédération Général du Travail*), had been split in two in 1921 when the communists led out a number of unions to form the CGTU (*Confédération Général du Travail Unitaire*); there were also divisions with the two groups, primarily between the revolutionary syndicalists and the reformists in the CGT and between the "one hundred per cent" communists, the communists of varying degrees of persuasion, the Trotskyites, the socialists, and others in the CGTU. (Simone Weil herself joined the Teachers' Union in the CGT on her arrival in Le Puy and a few months later also joined the Teachers' Federation of the CGTU, probably in order to be able to work within both groups.)

Seeing the trade unions as the natural job-oriented basis for worker organization and education, Weil believed that political differences should be subordinated to the major task of building an effective, politically independent trade union organization. However, the leaders of both the CGT and CGTU had just rejected a proposal for a merger; if unity were to come, she recognized, it would have to happen through the efforts of the rank and file. She felt that unity was crucial and believed, even at this time (she would develop this idea with increasing vigor in 1932 and 1933), that the only real hope for the revolution lay in the workers themselves, not in the trade union leaders.

She realized that the workers were not in any condition to assume the responsibilities of leadership. First and foremost, she thought, they needed to be freed from the domination of the intellectuals and given the "ability to handle language and especially the written language."[7] "At all times," whe wrote, "the ability to handle words has seemed to men something miraculous." It is one of the primary forms of power, and its exclusive possession by one group results in the "domination of those who know how to handle words over those who know how to handle things," a domination that is "rediscovered at every stage of human history."[8] The elimination of this split between thinkers and workers was, to her, the most important goal of the proletarian revolution; the revolution, in her eyes, did not mean the workers' taking possession of the means of production so much as their taking possession of, claiming as their own, the entire heritage of human thought. "Indeed," she wrote, "this act of taking possession is the revolution."[9] As a start in this direction, she supported a project to reinstitute classes for workers at the St.-Étienne Labor Exchange; beginning in December, she offered a French course to improve the workers' command of the written language and, in conjunction with another teacher, a course on political economy. Beginning in March, she also gave a course on Marx for the workers in Le Puy, at their request.

At this point in her life Simone Weil valued Marx primarily for his attempt to develop a scientific method of social analysis, though other of his ideas were important to her, particularly his perception of the essential injustice of capitalism. "As Marx forcibly showed," she wrote in 1933, "the very essence of the capitalist system consists . . . of a 'reversal of the relationship between subject and object,' a reversal brought about by the subordination of subject to object, of 'the worker to the material conditions of work'; and the revolution can have no other meaning except to restore to the thinking subject his proper relationship to matter, by giving him back the control which it is his function to exercise over it." (33 OL) However, she did not believe that the revolution could be accomplished simply by expropriating the means of production; it was the conditions of production themselves that were oppressive, conditions that were attendant upon mechanization and big industry. Elimination of capitalists and transfer of the ownership of the factories to the proletariat would do nothing in itself to change a system of production in which the human worker was the slave of the machine.

This need for a change in the whole orientation of machine technology had been brought home to her forcibly when she made a visit to a small mine in the St.-Étienne region in March 1932. Weil asked to be allowed to use the compressed-air drill, and she tried to replicate for herself the miners' experience of the machine by applying herself to it to the limit of her strength. Pétrement reports that if her friends had not stopped her, "she would have kept on using the air drill until she had collapsed."[10] In an article that appeared the following week in a regional trade union newspaper, she explored the philosophical and human implications of the technology that created the compressed-air drill, a technology that as she saw it radically and destructively changed the proper relationship between man and the world:

At present the drama is no longer played out between the coal and the man but between the coal and the compressed air. It is the compressed air that, at the accelerated tempo that is its proper tempo, drives the point of the pickax into the wall of coal, and stops, and then drives again. Forced to intervene in this struggle between gigantic forces, man is crushed. Clinging to the pickax or drill, his entire body being shaken, like the machine, by the rapid vibrations of compressed air, he confines himself to keeping the machine applied at each instant to the wall of coal, in the required position. . . . he forms a single body with the machine and is added to it like a supplementary gear, vibrating in time with its incessant shaking. This machine is not modeled on human nature but rather on the nature of coal and compressed air, and its movements follow a rhythm profoundly alien to the rhythm of life's movements, violently bending the human body to its service.[11]

Such a technology, as the image in the last line so vividly suggests, is dehumanizing in the extreme. As long as it remained unchanged, Weil was convinced, oppression would continue unchanged, no matter what revolutionary political and economic changes might take place. "The political and economic revolutions will become real," she wrote, "only if they are extended into a technical revolution that will re-establish, within the mine and the factory, the domination that it is the worker's function to exercise over the conditions of work."[12]

It is clear that at this point Simone Weil was not thinking of the proletarian revolution as something merely theoretically possible, which might emerge at some distant time in the future, but as something at the very door. There is an unmistakable urgency in both her work and her writing, an urgency in the questions she asks, an urgency in her adjurations to her comrades to organize, to think, to study the situation, to prepare the proletariat for the task of governing. And she expected the Soviet Union, as the "international fatherland of the workers," to be actively supportive of the revolution as it emerged in Europe.

However, with the death of Lenin and the coming to power of Stalin in 1927, the Russia of the October Revolution had begun to change its orientation. Trotsky, who advocated "permanent revolution," was forced into exile, and Stalin pursued a policy of developing socialism in a single state—from which, once it had been successfully achieved, it would be exported to the waiting workers of the world. Stalin launched the first Five Year Plan (1928) to rapidly industrialize Russia, a process which also demanded bureaucratic control over every aspect of the economy and imposed on the Russian workers the same oppressive conditions which the revolution was supposed to have ended. There was no private ownership of industrial property, but the state itself was filling the role of the oppressor. In foreign policy, too, Russia was changing its image and trying to put to rest the capitalist world's fears of an aggressive and expanding Bolshevism. The Soviet Union needed peace with the

outside world in order to carry out its great internal projects, and in February 1932, at the World Conference for
Disarmament, the Russian Commissar of Foreign Af-
fairs, Maxim Litvinov, proclaimed Russia's desire to collaborate with the capitalist states in the interest of peace.

Much earlier than most of the European left, Simone
Weil began to look critically at developments in Russia
and to question publically whether Russian policies were
intended to further socialism at home and abroad or to
create a powerful Russian state. To Weil, Russia's pro-
fessed desire to collaborate with the capitalist nations
seemed a betrayal of the world proletariat, all the more
so because it came at a time when the economic crisis
in Europe had created truly revolutionary conditions. In
Germany, where the economic crisis was most acute, a
revolution of some sort, either of the right or of the left,
seemed imminent; Trotsky, writing on the German situation in January 1932,[13] had warned that if the Communist Party persisted in its do-nothing attitude, it would
only bring about the defeat of the German working class
without a battle and would guarantee the triumph of fascism. Weil, in a commentary on Trotsky's article, predicted that Germany's resolution of the problem would
be crucial for all of Europe. A proletarian revolution in
Germany would give new impetus to the Russian revolution, perhaps to the point of breaking the oppressive
hold of the Stalinist bureaucracy; on the other hand, a
fascist Germany would form a bloc with fascist Italy and
give strength to the fascist currents in the rest of Europe.[14]

Germany's early industrialization and its large and
well-disciplined working class gave it, in the thinking of
many revolutionary theorists, perhaps the most favorable
conditions of any European country for the development
of a victorious proletarian revolution. The syndicalist
movement was strong and well organized; its leadership,
however, was almost entirely reformist, being closely
tied to the Social Democratic Party, which in turn was

tied to the political and economic structure of the Weimar Republic. In the mid- to late 1920s, when Germany was relatively prosperous, the Social Democrats had done very well by the workers, but with the coming of the Depression things had changed radically, and by the summer of 1932 Germany was in the midst of a staggering political and economic crisis.

The need for strong governmental action to cope with the crisis led the president of the republic to grant emergency powers to the chancellor to govern by decree rather than through the usual parliamentary methods. Democratic government was suspended, and intrigues were afoot within the government to keep it so permanently and place power in the hands of one of several competing rightist aspirants. This governmental crisis was complicated by the bid for power of Hitler and his Nazi party. Appealing to German nationalism, chauvinism, and anti-Semitism, taking advantage of the fear caused by the economic crisis and the resentment many Germans felt at the limitations placed on Germany's size and military strength by the treaty of Versailles, he promised a powerful Third Reich, an expansive, triumphant Germany, and a "new order" of strength, superiority, and security. The elections of July 1932 had given his Nazi party two hundred and thirty seats in the Reichstag, making it the largest single party, and Hitler was exerting all his considerable tactical skill to have himself appointed chancellor with full dictatorial powers.

In August 1932 Simone Weil went to Germany to see for herself what the situation was like. She found that the severity of the economic crisis had made the dependence of the individual on the social system a painful and unavoidable reality for large numbers of people. There was widespread fear and insecurity, and the unemployed—nearly half of the working class—felt that their lives and hopes had been crushed. To Weil, the crisis clearly showed that the capitalist system did not regard

men as human beings but only as tools which were left
to rust when they were not needed. It also seemed obvious
to her that the crisis was a propitious time for revolution;
the unemployed, at least, had nothing to lose. But the
unemployed lacked both the morale and the leadership
to bring down the old system, and the workers' organizations, which should have provided the leadership, were
for various reasons doing nothing.

Weil returned to France and subsequently wrote
more than a dozen articles analyzing the situation in Germany.[15] Her initial guarded optimism that perhaps the
moment was coming when "the working class will appear
in its strength, with more éclat than in Paris in 1871, or
in St. Petersburg in 1905" (142 EHP) was succeeded by
an increasing certainty that the workers would go under
without a struggle. Her admiration for the German workers and for their level of culture and their spirit was
enormous; she attributed their passivity to the demoral-
ization caused by the years of unemployment, but she
laid the real responsibility for their weakness as a political
force at the doors of the workers' organizations. The
syndicalist organization—very strong, with four million
members—was allied with the Social Democratic Party,
and its leadership had found itself a secure and even
relatively powerful place within the existing political-
economic structure; it was pursuing socialism through
state control of the economy rather than through a transformation of the system that would result in democratic
worker control.

Simone Weil was even more critical of the German
Communist Party. Although there was some display of
revolutionary energy among the rank and file, and though
there had been a few spontaneous efforts on the part of
the ranks to form a united front with the socialist workers,
the communist leadership, acting on orders from Moscow, sat back and did nothing. The spontaneous movements, lacking direction and organization, petered out

ineffectively. Weil was astonished and then dismayed at the German Communist Party's inertness; by October 1932 she had concluded that "the German Communist party is not the organization of German workers resolved to prepare the transformation of the regime...it is a propaganda organization in the hands of the bureaucratic Russian State." (138 EHP) The needs of Russian foreign policy were being put before the needs of the German workers; a fascist Germany would crush the workers' movement, but the Russian state was not at that point convinced that a fascist Germany would not be in some ways advantageous to itself. Moreover, a serious revolutionary movement in Germany would give considerable strength to the leftist opposition in Russia in its struggle against the bureaucratic dictatorship. "It is thus natural," Weil wrote drily, "that the Russian bureaucracy subordinates everything, even at this tragic moment, to the need to maintain its grip on the German revolutionary movement." (138 EHP)

It might have been "natural" for the Russian state to behave as it did, but Weil was far from calm about that fact or about its implications. Despite communist propaganda to the effect that fascism was simply the last stage of a dying capitalism that would soon give way before a victorious proletariat, she began to perceive that the kind of political structure that was emerging in Europe in the 1930s was something totally different from anything Marx had foreseen. Marx had predicted that the very structures of capitalism would give rise to a proletarian class that would ultimately take the privately owned means of production into its own hands and usher in the final stage of history in which there would be no division of men into producers and exploiters, oppressed and oppressors. But in Russia, where capitalism had been overthrown fifteen years previously, there was no sign of a social structure based on the democratic cooperation of the workers; instead, the workers were economically and politically at the mercy of an oppressive and dictatorial state. And this same structure of state control was rapidly taking shape in Germany under Hitler.

Weil stated this problem in a vigorous essay called "Prospects: Are We Heading for the Proletarian Revolution?"[16] which was published in the revolutionary syndicalist journal *La Révolution Prolétarienne* in August 1933. She began by observing that although capitalism had apparently reached the limits beyond which it could no longer expand, there were fewer signs than ever of the advent of socialism. What was appearing, she argued, was a new system of oppression in which the dominant class was no longer made up of the capitalists who owned the means of production but of the bureaucrats, technicians, and managers who, as industry grew larger and more centralized, exercised the all-important function of planning and coordinating the work to be done.

Marx had seen that the socialization of labor created through large-scale capitalism enormously increased productivity and therefore made possible the conditions of material abundance necessary for a socialist society in which all would be equal and all would have enough. He was not unaware of the oppressive power of bureaucracies, but he believed that this was a secondary problem that would disappear along with capitalism. However, fifty years after the death of Marx, it was evident to Simone Weil that bureaucracy was not a secondary problem but was tied in to the very technological advances that increased productivity. These advances in methods of production carried in their wake two factors that militated against the emergence of a society in which there would no longer be a "degrading division between intellectual and manual work" and in which the worker would be the master of the machine, not its servant. The very methods that increased productivity—the division

and specialization of labor and the reduction of the worker's task to simple and repetitive movements—deepened
the split between intellectual and manual labor by making
the worker little more than a machine tender who was
given no scope for the use of intelligence, initiative, and
creativity in his work. These same methods of production
also created the conditions which made inevitable the
growth of a management class responsible for overseeing
and coordinating the work of large numbers of unskilled
or semiskilled workers. Insofar as the managers and co-
ordinators were responsible for the actual operation of
the means of production, theirs was the most important
function, and they were becoming, therefore, the dominant class. Instead of leading inevitably toward socialism, as Marx had argued, industrial capitalism had
engendered another—and potentially even more inhuman—system of oppression.

The prospects for changing this direction seemed
poor. Weil had always looked to the skilled workers and
to the workers' organizations to provide the foundation
for the building of a new society, but the techniques of
modern industry were eliminating skilled workers, and
the workers' organizations themselves ran the risk in-
herent in any large organization of developing a bureaucracy. Nevertheless, she did not intend to give up; while
it seemed that there was little that could be done, that
little, she insisted, should be done. And at the conclusion
of her pessimistic analysis as to the likelihood of success
was a refusal to be morally defeated:

The powerful forces that we have to fight are preparing to crush
us; and it is true that they can prevent us from existing fully,
that is to say from stamping the world with the seal of our will.
But there is one sphere in which they are powerless. They
cannot stop us from working towards a clear comprehension
of the object of our efforts, so that, if we cannot accomplish
what we will, we may at least have willed it, and not just have

blindly wished for it; and, on the other hand, our weakness may indeed prevent us from winning, but not from comprehending the force by which we are crushed. Nothing in the world can prevent us from thinking clearly. (23 OL)

3

1933–1934

In the autumn of 1933, Simone Weil was posted to the girls' lycée in Roanne, about seventy-five kilometers north of St.-Étienne (she had requested Roanne in order to be within reasonable traveling distance of her revolutionary syndicalist comrades in St.-Étienne). In the Roanne lycée she enjoyed for the first time a relatively harmonious relationship with the school administration. In Le Puy her activities on behalf of the town's unemployed—she had led a delegation of unemployed workers to the city council, among other things—had generated considerable uproar, and pressure had been brought to bear on her to request an administrative transfer in the middle of the school year. She finished the year, however, and accepted a transfer to Auxerre, a town in a wine-producing region about one-hundred-sixty kilometers south of Paris, for the year 1932–33. Her relationship with the administration in Auxerre was not good; according to Pétrement, rather than have Simone Weil return the following year, the headmistress abolished the philosophy class.[1] In Roanne, although her unusual teaching methods were met by some administrative opposition—there is mention of some scenes that took place when the headmistress came looking "for marks and positions which Simone Weil usually refused to give"[2]—these differences were apparently resolved amicably. Her situation in Roanne seems to have been in many senses ideal. The class, a student remembers,

was a small one and had a family atmosphere about it: housed apart from the main school buildings, in a little summer house almost lost in the school grounds, we made our first acquaintance with great thoughts in an atmosphere of complete independence. When the weather was good we had our lessons under the shade of a fine cedar tree, and sometimes they became a search for the solution to a problem in geometry, or a friendly conversation.[3]

(One might be reminded of Plato teaching his students in the grove of Akadēmos—an image that must also have occurred to Simone Weil, for she wrote over the door of the little summer house that was her classroom the same Greek inscription that adorned the lintel of Plato's school: "No one admitted unless he knows geometry.")

Accurate and detailed notes of Simone Weil's lectures at Roanne were taken by a student and published as *Leçons de philosophie* in 1959 (English translation, *Lectures on Philosophy*, 1978). Because Weil alternates the views of the major philosophical and social thinkers who were the staples of her education with her own present angle of concern on philosophical, social, and political problems, the *Lectures* provide an invaluable record both of her training and of the way she was modifying it in the formation of her own views, particularly in politics and sociology. The text also clearly shows the connections between Weil's epistemological and social/political thought and the relationship of both to her conception of what it is to be human. Leading her students through the basic problems in philosophy, she emphasized that the specific dignity of the human being is reason, the capacity to think, and that the proper exercise of the mind develops both consciousness—the ability to think and to know the world—and conscience, the awareness of value. As the lectures unfold, the core of her thinking on the relationship between the mind, the world, and work becomes evident; she describes the discovery of necessity—a network of necessary relationships—that is a result of the mind's encounter with the obstacle presented by the material world. This chain of relationships, this necessary order, she suggests, is nothing other than the essence of thought itself. Matter, that which is by definition not mind, utterly different from mind, is thus that through which the essential character of mind is revealed. Relating this idea to the actual working conditions in industrial society in the section of the lectures on politics and social theory, Weil emphasized how modern industrial conditions destroy work as an exercise of thought and make human work literally mechanical. Workers are treated as mere material objects, not thinking beings, and human value and human dignity are both destroyed.

The lectures also reflect Weil's preoccupation with the problem of discovering the causes of social oppression. Like Marx, she saw the methods of production as the crucial determinants of the shape of any given society, but unlike him, she saw no reason to believe that the increase in productivity brought about by capitalism and the development of big industry would continue indefinitely and lead to a state of utopian socialism in which work would be virtually unnecessary. Rather, as she had argued in "Prospects" and as she taught her students, Weil saw big industry itself as the heart of the problem. The centralization, division of labor, and specialization that make big industry possible also create conditions that tend only to intensify, not to eliminate, what is most destructive in the capitalist system—the reversal of the relationship between subject and object, ends and means. Weil became increasingly concerned with the direction she saw being taken by current political and economic trends and increasingly convinced that Marxist thought was inadequate to explain it; toward the end of the year, when her students were occupied with reading for their examinations, she began to compose a long essay summing up the agonies of the present situation and asking what, if any, real hope there was for improvement. She worked with great intensity on this essay—which she jokingly referred to as her "magnum opus"—for several months. (It remained unpublished during her lifetime. It was first published in 1955 under the title *"Réflexions sur les causes de la liberté et de l'oppression sociale"* in the collection *Oppression et liberté* and appears in English translation in *Oppression and Liberty* [1958].)

"Reflections Concerning the Causes of Liberty and Social Oppression" is a measured, profound, and often extraordinarily beautiful meditation on the nature of modern industrial civilization. Nearly one hundred pages long and very tightly written, it is divided into four parts: a critique of Marxism, an analysis of oppression, a theoretical picture of a free society, and, in contrast to that ideal, a sketch of the actual reality of contemporary social life. It begins with a brief introductory statement of the problem as it was reflected in 1934. First, the psychological and personal value of work has been undermined; because of unemployment, work is "no longer done with the proud consciousness that one is being useful, but with the humiliating and agonizing feeling of enjoying a privilege from which one excludes several human beings by the mere fact that one enjoys, in short, a job." (37 OL) Second, technological progress has failed to produce a prosperous and happy society. Third, Enlightenment hopes that the growth of scientific knowledge would lead to the diffusion of knowledge and the development of the powers of thought in the masses of the population have been proved false. Fourth, art suffers, because of the reciprocal relation between art and society; and finally, the whole of humanity feels that it is "living through a period bereft of a future," for the future "is no longer a matter of hope, but of anguish." (38 OL) The one hope—the "magic word" which since 1789 has "contain[ed] within itself all imaginable futures"—has been revolution, but in the present, revolution, too, seems in reality to be an empty word: "We ought, so it seems, to be in a period of full revolution; but in fact everything goes on as if the revolutionary movement were falling into decay with the very system it aspires to destroy." (38 OL)

Since it is Marxist theory that provided the primary buttresses for revolutionary hopes by supposedly demonstrating "the ineluctable necessity of an early upheaval, in which the oppression we suffer under capitalism would be abolished," Weil begins the body of her essay with a critique of Marxism. The expectation of a revolutionary upheaval has been accepted as a dogma, but it has not, she argues, been examined closely; examining it, she finds that it contains many difficulties. Capitalist oppression of the workers does not have as its primary objective the extortion of surplus value for the capitalists' own consumption but rather for the expansion of the enterprise "as rapidly as possible so as to make it more powerful than its rivals." (40 OL) The struggle for power, Weil argues, necessitates the continuing oppression of the working masses: "so long as there is, on the surface of the globe, a struggle for power, and as long as the decisive factor in victory is industrial production, the workers will be exploited." Marx assumed that the struggle for power would disappear when socialism was established in all industrialized countries. The trouble with this assumption, Weil points out, is that "revolution cannot take place everywhere at once; and when it does take place in one country, it does not for that country do away with the need for exploiting and oppressing the mass of workers, but on the contrary accentuates the need, lest it be found weaker than the other nations. The history of the Russian

Revolution furnishes a painful illustration of this." (40 OL)

Moreover, Weil reiterates, the solution to the problem is not the abolition of private property, because the source of oppression does not lie in the system of private property but in the modern system of production itself, which, because it subordinates the workers to the machine and to the undertaking as a whole, is by its very nature oppressive. The specialization fostered by the modern industrial system "implies the enslavement of those who execute to those who co-ordinate"; a society based on specialization "can only organize and perfect oppression, not lighten it." (40 OL) Weil therefore disputes the Marxist assumption that capitalism would develop within itself the material conditions necessary for the establishment of a free and egalitarian society; on the contrary, she argues, the establishment of a regime of liberty and equality "presupposes a preliminary transformation in both production and culture." (63 OEL; cf. 42 OL)

The second section, "Analysis of Oppression," is an attempt to grasp the mechanism of oppression, to understand "by what means it arises, subsists, transforms itself, [and] by what means, perhaps, it might theoretically disappear." (56–7 OL) Marx's analysis of oppression, she argues, "only partially describes its origins" and does not explain oppression. In her own analysis, which constitutes the bulk of this section, Weil finds that oppression begins when society moves from a primitive state in which each person or family is engaged in wresting food, clothing, shelter, etc., directly from nature to a more complex state in which methods of production are sufficiently improved so that surplus goods are stored up and systematic coordination, both of workers and of the products of work, becomes more and more necessary. It can be seen historically, she observes, that all societies which know how to produce surplus goods are organized in an oppressive way.

She makes a fundamental distinction between the struggle against nature (i.e., the struggle for subsistence) and the struggle against other men; though the latter is related to the struggle for subsistence, its original end (a better living) is soon lost sight of in the struggle for power for its own sake that ensues. This factor—the struggle for power over other men—Weil saw as the root of the problem of social oppression. Because of the very nature of human beings, power over them can never be stable, and hence can never be held securely:

men are essentially active beings and have a faculty of self-determination which they can never renounce, even should they so desire, except on the day when, through death, they drop back into the state of inert matter; so that every victory won over men contains within itself the germ of a possible defeat, unless it goes as far as extermination. But extermination abolishes power by abolishing its object. There is thus, in the very essence of power, a fundamental contradiction that prevents it from ever existing in the true sense of the word. (67 OL)

Once the methods of production are sufficiently advanced that men are divided into those who command and those who carry out orders, those who command have a position of power to protect, and the vicious circle of the power struggle begins. Weil's description of the madness of this phenomenon is profound and beautiful:

the race for power enslaves everybody, strong and weak alike. Marx saw this clearly with reference to the capitalist system. Rosa Luxemburg used to inveigh against the aspect of "aimless merry-go-round" presented by the Marxist picture of capitalist accumulation, that picture in which consumption appears as a "necessary evil" to be reduced to the minimum, as a mere means for keeping alive those who devote themselves, whether as leaders or workers, to the supreme object, which is none other than the manufacture of capital equipment, that is to say of the means of production. And yet it is the profound absurdity of this picture which gives it its profound truth; a truth which extends singularly beyond the framework of the capitalist system. The only characteristic peculiar to this system is that the instruments of industrial production are at the same time the chief weapons in the race for power; but always the methods pursued in the race for power, whatever they may be, bring men under their subjection through the same frenzy and impose themselves on them as absolute ends. (68 OL)

The methods pursued in the race for power bring men under their subjection and impose themselves on them as absolute ends. The substitution of means for ends, Weil suggests, is a reversal of a moral order so profound that the inevitable consequences are the moral and often physical destruction of all concerned. Those who pursue power as an end come, as much as those whom they oppress, to be blindly dominated by the very machinery of the pursuit of power, whether that machinery be war, production, or wealth.

Weil saw this strange and generally uncomprehended domination of the powerful by the very instruments of domination they wielded reflected in the earliest masterpiece of Western literature. The "real subject of the *Iliad*," she writes in this essay, "is the sway exercised by war over the warriors... none of them knows why each sacrifices himself and all his family to a bloody and aimless war, and this is why, all through the poem, it is the gods who are credited with the mysterious influence which nullifies peace negotiations.... Thus in this ancient and wonderful poem there already appears the essential evil besetting humanity, the substitution of means for ends." (68 OL) This substitution, she goes on, is a "fundamental folly that accounts for all that is senseless and bloody right through history."

Human history is simply the history of the servitude which makes men—oppressors and oppressed alike—the plaything of the instruments of domination they themselves have manufactured, and thus reduces living humanity to being the chattel of inanimate chattels. (69 OL)

If this is indeed the way the social mechanism operates, is there any possibility that human societies can enjoy a high level of production and not inevitably generate oppressive social structures? Looking at societies as they actually existed, Weil was inclined to say no; indeed, the section of the essay subtitled "Analysis of Oppression" concludes, "It would seem that man is born a slave, and that servitude is his natural condition." (83 OL) Immediately, however, at the beginning of "Theoretical Picture of a Free Society," she follows this statement with a tremendous affirmation based on the fact that man is not only a creature subject to material forces but also a thinking being: "nothing on earth can stop man from feeling himself born for liberty. Whatever may happen, he can never accept servitude; for he is a thinking creature." (113 OEL; cf. 83 OL)

Here again Simone Weil's conception of the relationship between the knower and the known—the mind and the world—is basic to her social theory. In her view, the relationship between the mind and the world is established by the human being's capacity for thought and action, by means of which the mind encounters, knows, and changes the world. Like the materialists, Marx and Darwin in particular, she saw man as a part of nature, rooted in nature, subject to the material conditions of his existence; yet inasmuch as he "exercises a free activity," she saw man (as she argued Marx did also) as radically separate from nature, "an antagonistic term *vis-a-vis* nature." (32 OL) She sought a synthesis of idealism and materialism, arguing that reality exists neither in the mind alone nor in matter alone but in the contact between them made possible by thought. It exists "in the act by which thinking man takes possession of the world." (33 OL) This relationship between the mind and the world is absolutely fundamental in Weil's thinking. It is given, and it is normative; any social organization which distorts or destroys it is unsound in the most fundamental way.

The ideal relationship between mind and body, man and universe, is a "happy balance." The division of labor which separates men into those who plan and those who carry out orders destroys this balance between thought and action in the individual; it also "give[s] birth to a false conception of the relationship between man and nature, from the mere fact that it is only the downtrodden who are in direct contact with nature, that is to say those who are excluded from theoretical culture, deprived of the right of and opportunity for self-expression." (30 OL) Both oppressors and oppressed suffer in a social structure which fragments their wholeness as beings who think *and* act and drives a wedge between their thought and its proper object.

This fragmentation is not, Weil argues, confined to the division of labor in industry but is characteristic of modern civilization as a whole. Specialization in industry has enormously increased productivity, and specialization in intellectual fields has enormously increased the sum total of human knowledge, but in both cases at the price of reducing the individual to the status of a cog in a vast machine. Insofar as a body of knowledge is too large to be grasped by the individual mind, the individual is subordinated to it, and the proper relationship between the thinking subject and the object of thought is inverted: "where the mind cannot embrace everything, it must necessarily play a subordinate role." (94 OL) The maintenance of the proper relationship between the mind and its object, Weil argues, is of far greater importance than the piling up of knowledge: "it would be enough if man were no longer to aim at extending his knowledge and power indefinitely, but rather at establishing, both in his search and in his work, a certain balance between the mind and the objects to which it is being applied." (95–96 OL) Without this balance, she insists, real thought is not possible: "Thought is certainly man's supreme dignity, but it is exercised in a vacuum, and consequently only in appearance, when it does not seize hold of its object, which can be none other than the universe." (105 OL)

The absence of real thought, she argues, is a profoundly disturbing characteristic of modern civilization: "never have men been less capable, not only of subordinating their actions to their thoughts, but even of thinking.... In appearance, nearly everything nowadays is carried out methodically; science is king.... But in reality methodical thought is progressively disappearing, owing to the fact that the mind finds less and less matter on which to bite." (108–9 OL) For instance, she contends, the enormous progress made in modern mathematics has been an unbalanced progress achieved through the manipulation of algebraic signs whose original relationship to things in the world has been increasingly lost sight of: "The signs combine together according to the laws governing the things which they signify; but, for want of being able to keep the relationship of sign to thing signified continually present to the mind, one handles them as though they combined together according to their own laws; and as a result the combinations become unintelligible, which means to say that they take place automatically." (93 OL)

When the mind no longer has the world as its object, the idea of necessity is lost. This term—necessity—is extremely important in Weil's thinking. She sometimes uses it in a rather broad way to refer to the world as obstacle, as antagonistic matter, as that which is foreign to us and indifferent to our will. Using the word in this sense, she writes, "The pressure of necessity weighs continually upon us; as long as man goes on existing, that is to say as long as he continues to constitute an infinitesimal fraction in this pitiless universe, the pressure exerted by necessity will never be relaxed for one single moment. A state of things in which man had as much enjoyment and as little fatigue as he liked can, except in fiction, find no place in the world in which we live." (84 OL)

Weil also understands necessity not as matter, as obstacle in all its density, but as a web of relationships governing the behavior of matter. It is only because of these stable patterns of relationship that methodical action in the world is possible; in a world in which matter appeared as pure chaos or entirely dominated by chance, human beings would be able to act only blindly and randomly; work, in the sense that Weil uses the term, could not exist.

The perception of necessity is of moral as well as epistemological importance. The man of power, the man whose wishes are carried out by slaves, is able to avoid to a large degree the knowledge of the existence of an inexorable and resistant world. Consequently, there is no check on his desires; he enjoys the illusion of a greater freedom than other men, but in reality he is a victim of his own capricious passions; he is "prey to desires to which the clear perception of necessity never comes to assign any limit." (96 OL) For the human being to become what he should be, the encounter with necessity is a sine qua non: "the source of any kind of virtue lies in the shock produced by the human intelligence being brought up against a matter devoid of lenience and of falsity. It is not possible to conceive of a nobler destiny for man than that which brings him directly to grips with naked necessity, without his being able to expect anything except through his own exertions, and such that his life is a continual creation of himself by himself." (87 OL)

The encounter with necessity is the substance of work. Work, thus, is a source of human value; it is the means by which the human being modifies and therefore to some degree creates the conditions of his existence and to that degree creates himself. Through the "effort demanded in overcoming external obstacles," it gives him the discipline necessary for self-mastery—the subordi-

nation of his passions to his thought—and thus enables
him to establish the proper relationship between his mind
and his body, his mind and the world. The real exigencies
of work are of such value that they are imitated in activities defined as the opposite of work, e.g., art and
sport: "Even the apparently freest forms of activity, science, art, sport, only possess value in so far as they
imitate the accuracy, rigour, scrupulousness which characterize the performance of work, and even exaggerate
them." (85 OL)

Work and the conception of necessity which is inseparable from it also provide the structure within which
liberty can be defined. Liberty understood as freedom
from any restriction is a fantasy, for it has no connection
with the real conditions of human existence and therefore,
Weil insists, can have no value or meaning: "If one were
to understand by liberty the mere absence of all necessity,
the word would be emptied of all concrete meaning; but
it would not then represent for us that which, when we
are deprived of it, takes away the value from life." (85
OL) Liberty, then, involves the freedom to bring the mind
to grips with necessity; and this is nothing other than to
work, if work is understood not as the carrying out of
another's will but the application of one's own thought
with a view to effecting changes in the world.

Given this relationship between work and liberty,
work and thought, work and knowledge, Weil concludes
that the "most fully human civilization would be that
which had manual labour as its pivot, that in which manual labour constituted the supreme value." (104 OL) In
such an ideal civilization, labor would no longer be valued primarily in terms of its products but in terms of its
relation to the person who performs it; it would "constitute for each human being what he is most essentially in
need of if his life is to take on of itself a meaning and a
value in his own eyes." (104 OL) In other words, in
work, in the encounter with the real conditions of human

existence, one finds the meaning of what it is to be human; and this experience, Weil believed, was the foundation for a truly human, that is to say, a thinking and value-oriented, life.

The idea of labor as a human value was, Weil believed, the only truly new idea that had emerged in Western thought since ancient times. The old conception, reflected in the Genesis story, makes labor a punishment for sin; it makes "the world appear as a penitentiary and labor as the sign of men's servitude and abasement." (140 OEL; cf. 106 OL) At the beginning of the Renaissance, Weil argues, Francis Bacon conceived a new relation between man and the world when he wrote that "We cannot command nature except by obeying her." (106–7 OL) Through this statement Bacon was generalizing the idea that by thought, by the understanding of the necessary laws governing the physical world—by "obeying" nature, in other words—human beings can turn the forces of nature to their own use. Thus, the pilot, by means of rudder, tiller, and sail, can use the wind to move his boat in the opposite direction from that in which the wind is blowing. In a manner of speaking, he "commands" the forces of nature.

Following this change in the conception of the human relationship to nature, Weil notes, there emerged in post-Renaissance literature the ideal "of a life devoted to some free form of physical labour." It is evident, she points out, at the end of Goethe's *Faust*, in which Faust "longs to be stripped of his magic power" and exclaims, "'If I could stand before thee, Nature, simply as a man, then it would be worth while being a human creature.'" (107 OL) Weil found it evident also in the works of Rousseau, Shelley, Tolstoy, Proudhon, and Marx, and in the nineteenth-century revolutionary syndicalists, who "place at the core of the social problem the dignity of the producer as such." (108 OL) In this conception of labor as a source of spiritual value. Weil believed, lay the real greatness and originality of modern civilization: "we may feel proud," she writes, "to belong to a civilization which has brought with it the presage of a new ideal."

However, she writes in the final section, "Sketch of Contemporary Social Life," despite the emergence of this new ideal, the actual form which modern civilization has assumed could not be more contrary to it. The reason, she contends, is that in its fascination with technical achievements, modern Western humanity has not taken into account the limitations and the scale of the human body; as a result, human beings are dwarfed, submerged, ground down by the magnitude of their own creations. There is an enormous disequilibrium between the human body (man's only mode of being in the world) and modern forms of economic and social organization: "We are living in a world in which nothing is made to man's measure; there exists a monstrous discrepancy between man's body, man's mind and the things which at the present time constitute the elements of human existence." This discrepancy is largely a matter of quantity, but at a certain point "quantity is changed into quality, as Hegel said, and in particular a mere difference in quantity is sufficient to change what is human into what is inhuman."

> ... certain units of measurement are given and have hitherto remained invariable, such as the human body, human life, the year, the day, the average quickness of human thought. Present-day life is not organized on the scale of all these things; it has been transported into an altogether different order of magnitude, as though man were trying to raise it to the level of the forces of outside nature while neglecting to take his own nature into account. (108–9 OL)

In consequence of this disregard of the scale on which it is possible for the individual to operate, the collectivity has usurped the function which belongs to the thinking individual:

To the very extent to which what is systematic in contemporary
life escapes the control of the mind, its regularity is established
by things which constitute the equivalent of what collective
thought would be if the collectivity did think. The cohesiveness
of science is ensured by means of signs. . . . In the sphere of
labour, the things which take upon themselves the essential
functions are machines. The thing which relates production to
consumption and governs the exchange of products is money.
Finally, where the function of co-ordination and management
is too heavy for the mind and intelligence of one man, it is
entrusted to a curious machine, whose parts are men, whose
gears consist of regulations, reports and statistics, and which
is called bureaucratic organization. (110 OL)

"Thus," she concludes, "in all spheres, thought, the prerogative of the individual, is subordinated to vast mechanisms which crystallize collective life. . . . The inversion
of the relation between means and ends—an inversion
which is to a certain extent the law of every oppressive
society—here becomes total or nearly so." (111 OL)

The collectivity, as Weil repeatedly insists, though
it operates as a sort of organizational nervous system for
the body politic, does not think; it is therefore incapable
of real judgments of value, which belong to thought alone.
As a result, in a mass society dominated by the collectivity, value is determined on the criterion of efficiency,
and judgment of value is thus "as it were entrusted to
material objects instead of to the mind." (113 OL) But
not only in judgments of value is the relationship between
thought and its object lost sight of; this phenomenon is
occurring in all spheres, with the result that order is
increasingly being replaced by chaos: "our civilization is
invaded by an ever-increasing disorder, and ruined by a
waste in proportion to that disorder." (113 OL)

Everything, Weil felt in 1934, was on a trajectory
toward the ultimate destructiveness of war. Capitalism,
which in its beginnings had been constructive at least to
the degree that it waged its struggle for power by building

up the forces of production, now carries on that power struggle in wasteful and destructive ways: "publicity, lavish display of wealth, corruption, enormous capital investments based almost entirely on credit, marketing of useless products by almost violent methods, speculations with the object of ruining rival concerns—all these tend to undermine the foundations of our economic life far more than to broaden them." (115 OL) The very attempts to bring order to this incipient chaos increases the ultimate potential for organized destructiveness; inasmuch as economic life and the business of credit and exchange have become so complicated that in order to function they need to be regulated by something other than a free-market economy, the state machine "must naturally be led sooner or later to take the main hand" in this regulation. (116 OL) But "since war is the recognized form of struggle for power when the competitors are States, every increase in the State's grip on economic life has the effect of orienting industrial life yet a little farther toward preparation for war; while, conversely, the ever-increasing demands occasioned by preparation for war help day by day to bring the all-round economic and social activities of each country more and more into subjection to the authority of the central power." Thus the pivot around which contemporary economic and political life revolves, she concludes, "is none other than preparation for war." Her vision of the predictable future was grim indeed: "Wars will bring in their train a frantic consumption of raw materials and capital equipment, a crazy destruction of wealth of all kinds that previous generations have bequeathed us. When chaos and destruction have reached the limit beyond which the very functioning of the economic and social organization becomes materially impossible, our civilization will perish." (116 OL)

It seemed to Weil that decentralization offered the only possibility of hope, but the cooperation necessary to bring it about was "impossible to imagine" in a civilization based on competition. (120 OL) Yet apart from such cooperation, "there is no means of stopping the blind trend of the social machine towards an increasing centralization, until the machine itself suddenly jams and flies into pieces." There was very little, she thought, that the individual qua individual could do. Nevertheless, she saw no reason for giving up in despair; rather, she seems to have needed to draw up this balance sheet so carefully in order to make it perfectly clear to herself that what she was going to do she would do without any expectation of its having any significant effect. Modern civilization— like a car driverless and out of control—might be doomed to crash; but even if there was no hope of preventing that, there was all the more reason to try to understand it, to draw up "an inventory of modern civilization," to make an analysis of what is human and inhuman in it, and theoretically at least to try "to discover the means whereby the former elements may be developed at the expense of the latter." (123 OL) The fact that such an analysis would in all likelihood "remain without influence on the future evolution of social organization" did not, in her eyes, deprive it of its value: "Only fanatics are able to set no value on their own existence save to the extent that it serves a collective cause." Moreover, to be indifferent to one's effect on the collective cause is the first step in freeing oneself from the domination of the collectivity: "to react against the subordination of the individual to the collectivity implies that one begins by refusing to subordinate one's own destiny to the course of history." (124 OL) Thus, despite the pessimism of her historical prognosis, Weil concluded her "Reflections Concerning the Causes of Liberty and Social Oppression" on a note of high affirmation of the power of thought. To undertake a critical analysis of modern civilization would in itself, she insisted, "enable him who did so to escape the contagion of folly and collective frenzy by reaffirming on his own account, over the head of the social idol, the original pact between the mind and the universe." (124 OL)

Simone Weil seems to be speaking in these pages of a purely theoretical analysis of the social system. However, consistent with her epistemology, she continued to carry on that analysis not by withdrawing from the world but by going out to encounter it in the most direct way possible, as a manual worker. (Her withdrawal, such as it was, was from political activity alone.) At the end of the 1933–34 school year she applied for a leave of absence from teaching. She worked on her long essay throughout the summer and autumn, and early in December she joined the ranks of the factory workers.

4

1935–1936

Through Boris Souvarine, a good friend and the editor of *La Critique Sociale*, Simone Weil had met Auguste Detoeuf, the managing director of the Alsthom Company, a Paris factory that made electrical machinery. Detoeuf, who was also a member of the group that later published the magazine *Nouveaux Cahiers*, was concerned, like her, with new ways of organizing industry and society.[1] Weil later described him as an "independent mind and a man of rare goodness." (91 L) He saw to it that she was hired as an unskilled worker in his factory. Intending to live as much like an ordinary worker as possible, she rented a room in the neighborhood of the factory and began work on December 4, 1934.

She placed two epigraphs at the head of the *Journal d'usine* she kept during her eight and a half months as a factory worker. The first, a quotation in Greek from the *Iliad*, alludes to the fate foreseen by Hector for his wife Andromache: she will be carried off as a slave to Argos and forced to do menial tasks against her will, "under the pressure of a harsh necessity." Such slavery, the epigraph implies, submitted to under the necessity of earning a living, is the actual experience of the modern industrial worker. In contrast, the second epigraph reflects Weil's conception of what work should be:

Not only let the workman know what he is making—but if possible let him *perceive the use* of it—let him perceive nature modified by him.

Let his own work be an *object of contemplation* for each person.

The *Journal d'usine* is, for the most part, a record of Weil's day-to-day experience in three different factories between December 1934 and August 1935.[2] The *Journal* records in a spare fashion the details, difficulties, frustrations, pains, and very rare joys of the work. Virtually everything in the factory, Weil found, conspired to dehumanize the unskilled worker, to reduce him or her from a complex being capable of thought, initiative, responsibility, understanding, sensitivity, and fellow feeling to a machine whose only advantage over machines made of metal was that he was capable of carrying out orders. Jobs were fragmented, and the worker had no knowledge of the whole finished product of which he made one of the parts; thus he had no feeling that he made some useful object but only that he made simple, repetitive, fast, and physically exhausting movements. The emphasis on speed and efficiency led to the elimination of all that was interesting in the work itself and reduced the motivation for work entirely to the need for pay. The unrelenting necessity to work at full speed—not only to bring one's pay up to a level at which it was possible to live but also not to fall below the minimum number of pieces per hour one had to produce in order not to be fired—forced the worker to strive for a pace more suitable to machines, which do not suffer fatigue, than to human beings. Moreover, to maintain the necessary speed, the worker's specifically human capacities had to be suppressed: "in order to 'make the grade' one has to repeat movement after movement faster than one can think, so that not only reflection but even day-dreaming is impossible. In front of his machine, the worker has to annihilate his soul, his thought, his feelings, everything, for eight hours a day." (22 L)

Unlike many critics of industrialism who saw the industrial devaluation of work as a consequence of mechanization, Weil was against the system of industrial organization but not antipathetic to machines per se. In the factory, she found "the machines themselves highly attractive and interesting." (12 L) In an essay[3] written in 1942 and based on her 1935 work experience, she discussed the advantages of versatile automatic machines which, by means of different cams, could be set up by the worker to carry out a number of different jobs. It was not the machine itself which she regarded as dehumanizing but the relationship between man and machine in which the human being was not the master but the servant: "They [the machines] are not for him a means of turning a piece of metal to a specified form; he is for them a means whereby they will be fed the parts for an operation whose relation to the ones preceding and the ones following remains an impenetrable mystery to him." (63 SWR) The primary evil of the factory system, which expresses itself in so many different ways, is not that the work is hard or monotonous but that it is set up in such a way as to gut it of all that makes it creative and meaningful. Given Weil's understanding of work as man's primary way of knowing himself and the world, as something that, though it involves hardship and difficulties to be overcome, is also accompanied by feelings of joy and accomplishment, the actual working conditions of a factory must have seemed almost diabolically perverse. Everything seemed designed to reduce the scope of the worker's consciousness to the bare minimum necessary for him to carry out orders and to make him as much of a thing "as it is possible for a human creature to be." (60 SWR) In this Weil saw the very essence of slavery.

It was a slavery she not only observed but herself experienced to such a degree that it literally transformed her consciousness; she came to feel herself, even outside the factory, a slave. She found it, initially, inexpressible. In January 1935 she wrote to a friend of the impossibility of describing her factory experience: "at present it seems to me that I should need a new language to convey what needs to be said." (14 L) The humiliations of factory life, of which she speaks so bitterly in the 1936 letters, are symbols of the slavery that she knew so well but found so difficult to communicate in a way that someone who had not experienced it could understand. The particulars that she complains about may seem in themselves of small importance, but to her they carried a vast weight of meaning: "each physical annoyance needlessly imposed, each show of lack of respect, each brutality, each humiliation, however trivial, appears as a fresh reminder" to the worker that in the factory he or she, "though indispensable to the productive process, is accounted as practically nothing in it." (63 SWR)

After nearly eight months of total immersion in this life, Weil discovered that the experience had so penetrated her that even outside of work she had completely lost the feeling that she had any rights whatsoever. Getting on a bus one day in July, she found herself thinking with astonishment, "How is it that I, a slave, can get on this bus and for my 12 sous use it like anyone else? What an extraordinary favor! If I had been brutally made to get off, told that such comfortable means of travel were not for me, that I could go only on foot, I believe that that would have seemed to me entirely natural." Not to be treated brutally seemed purely gratuitous, like "a gift of chance." (124 CO)

Weil spent her last weeks at Renault in a state of physical and nervous exhaustion, plagued by headaches, outbreaks of eczema, and dizzy spells. "I got up with anguish, I went to the factory with fear, I worked like a slave," she wrote. (144 CO) She suffered "crushing, bitter fatigue, at times so painful that one wished for death. Everyone, in every situation, knows what it is to be fatigued, but for this fatigue there needs to be a separate name." (225–6 CO) She was able to stick it out for the length of time she had set for herself, but when she left Renault in August, she was in a "wretched state physically." In hopes of washing away "all this accumulated fatigue"[4] before returning to teaching in October, she took a freighter trip with her parents along the coast of Spain and also spent some time in Portugal. By the end of September she was back in Paris for a few days, and then she went to find a place to live in Bourges, a city about two hundred and fifty kilometers south of Paris, where she had been assigned a teaching post.

As it happened, one of her students in the Bourges lycée was the daughter of the owner of a foundry that manufactured stoves. Located in the countryside not far from Bourges, the Rosières Foundry employed about one thousand workers who with their families made up the population of the adjacent factory town.[5] Early in December an official visit to the factory was arranged, and Simone Weil, the headmistress of the lycée, the foundry owner's wife, son, and daughter, and some others were taken on a tour. On this visit Weil met the chief engineer and technical manager, a man named M. Bernard. She immediately began to challenge him about the inequalities between the workers' and managers' wages; before leaving, she made an appointment to talk to him the following week.

Weil met with Bernard a number of times between December 1935 and June 1936. She told him of her factory experiences, and they discussed the possibility of her being hired at some future time as a worker at Rosières. For the most part, however, her primary objective was communication; she wanted to learn more about the operation of the factory from the management's point of view, and she wanted to give Bernard the benefit of her knowledge of what it was like to be a worker. In general, she wrote him, she believed that one of the essential causes of human misery was that those in high places were not in a position to understand the condition of those at the bottom, and those at the bottom were not in a position to do anything about it. Having been at the bottom, she knew what it was like. "That is why," she wrote Bernard, "I so much want to be able to collaborate in some enterprise, from below, with the person who directs it." (183 CO; cf. 32 L)

It is clear from Simone Weil's correspondence with Bernard that her experience in the factory had reinforced the conclusion she had reached in 1934 that revolution would not solve the social problem. Her experience in the factory had taught her—much to her surprise—that what present industrial and economic conditions bred in fact was not rebellion but submission. Her association with both the working-class movement and the working masses of the Paris region had left her with the sad conviction that the "capacity of the French working class not only for revolution but for any action at all is almost nil." (37 L) And even if a working-class revolution were somehow to come about, she thought, it would not solve the problem, because it would not change the oppressive power relationships that were built into the present system of production: "After a so-called working-class revolution, just as much as before it, the workers at R. will go on obeying passively—so long as the system of production is based on passive obedience." (40 L)

Bernard had agreed to have Weil begin her "collaboration" with him by writing an article for *Entre Nous*, the newspaper he published for the workers. In the article she subsequently submitted to him, titled "An Appeal to the Workers at Rosières," she struck at what she felt was one of the most psychologically painful aspects of the moral submission demanded of the workers—the necessity of suppressing their feelings about their work and the way they were treated. She addressed the workers directly in her article; she frankly acknowledged that there might be "some days when you find it oppressive never to be able to say what you feel," and she encouraged them to put such feelings on paper and send them to her. She promised to edit them sufficiently to disguise the identity of the writers—in order to eliminate the workers' fear that there would be reprisals against them for saying what they felt—and to publish what they wrote in *Entre Nous*. In so addressing the workers as human beings who had feelings and a right to express them, she hoped to alleviate a little the "weight of humiliations which life inflicts every day upon the workers at R., as upon the workers in all modern factories." (24 L) She also hoped that ultimately *Entre Nous* could become a forum for real communication between workers and management: "By the scheme I am proposing you [the workers] might perhaps be able to make them [the managers] understand what at present they don't. . . . And perhaps they in turn will make use of *Entre Nous* to reply." (29 L) She made it clear that she did not expect major material changes to result from such communication: "Large-scale industry is what it is. The least one can say is that it imposes harsh living conditions. But neither you nor the employers will be able to change it in the near future." What might be changed were demoralizing conditions caused by ignorance and misunderstanding. She projected as a reasonable goal a compromise with economic necessity that was accompanied by understanding, forebearance, and goodwill on both sides:

The managers should understand exactly what is the life of the men they employ as hands. And their chief concern should be, not to be always trying to increase profit to the maximum, but to organize the most humane conditions of work that are compatible with whatever rate of profit is essential for the factory's existence.

The workers, on the other hand, should know and understand the necessities which control the factory's existence and their life in it. They would then be in a position to judge and appreciate the managers' goodwill. They would lose the sense of being always at the mercy of arbitrary commands, and the inevitable hardships would perhaps become less bitter to endure. (29 L)

Although Weil's proposal was in every respect moderate and uninflammatory, Bernard found the spirit of the article "shocking." He feared it would arouse discontent and exacerbate class feelings, and he refused to print it. In her subsequent correspondence with him, Weil defended her thinking and enlarged on her reasoning. The spirit of the article that he found so objectionable, she could not resist pointing out, was "purely and simply the Christian spirit." (23 L) Her aim in the article was simply, she said, to help the workers "to recover or retain, as the case may be, their sense of dignity." (24 L) That, she was convinced, was the necessary starting point "for any useful action affecting the mass of the people, and especially the factory workers." Beyond that, she hoped to see a gradual change "from total subordination to a certain mixture of subordination and co-operation, with complete co-operation as the ideal." (41 L)

Although Bernard spoke about collaboration with the workers, in Weil's eyes his idea of collaboration was inadequate because it did not touch the heart of the problem, that is, the power relationship between management and workers in which the workers were totally subordinate. "A spirit of collaboration," she wrote him, "calls for real collaboration; and at present I can discern nothing of that kind at R., but on the contrary a complete subordination." (41 L) The Rosières management, she granted, was benevolent and generous, but its very generosity to the workers only underlined management's active role and the workers' passive one. "Even their own Co-operative," she pointed out, "is not in fact controlled by them." (42 L) She repeatedly assured him that it was not subordination per se that she objected to but only subordination in which one human being was treated as a tool at the disposal of another or which suppressed the specifically human capacities of responsibility and intelligence: "there are circumstances in which subordination is something fine and honourable—for example: when orders confer a responsibility upon the recipient; when they make demands upon those virtues of courage, will, conscience, and intelligence which are the definition of human value; when they imply a certain mutual confidence between superior and subordinate and only a small degree of arbitrary power in the hands of the former." (47 L) But a situation "in which all the intelligence, ingenuity, will, and professional conscience are in the instructions elaborated by the superior, while the executant has only to obey passively," is totally dehumanizing; "in such a situation, the subordinate is almost like an inert object used as a tool by the intelligence of another."

Bernard, however, could not accept her arguments. He felt that she painted "too dark a picture of the moral conditions of the workers' life," and he was inclined to feel that she exaggerated or was hypersensitive. The more Weil told him of her painful experiences in the factory, the more he interpreted her reactions as evidence of a temperamental "hostility to superiors, envy of the more favoured, hatred of discipline, [and] continual discontent." (48 L) That, she countered, was not the case. She had, she wrote him, "to the highest degree a respect for discipline in work," and she was well aware "that all organization implies the giving and receiving of orders. But," she went on, "there are orders and orders," and in her experience as a worker the orders reinforced her awareness that she was regarded as a thing, and a thing, moreover, of no account. She reminded him how she had been "compelled by a foreman to work for two hours in a place where I was in danger of being knocked out by a swinging balance weight and thus made to feel for the first time how much I counted, i.e. not at all." (33 L) To react in a human way to this kind of treatment— to object to being treated as a thing, to express one's thoughts or one's feelings to a superior—was, she explained repeatedly, to risk at least a humiliating snub and even to risk being fired. The workers were reduced to a position in which the only way they could retain and affirm their humanity in their own eyes was to remain conscious of what they were undergoing, and to do so was unbearably painful.

Weil herself had managed to maintain a conscious existence during her time in the factory only at the cost of an extreme effort. "There came a day," she wrote Bernard early in their correspondence, "when I realized that a few weeks of that life had been almost enough to turn me into a docile beast of burden and that it was only on Sundays that I returned to something like a conscious life. I then asked myself with terror what I could become if it should ever happen that I was obliged to work in the same way seven days a week. I swore to myself that I would not give up until I had learned to live a worker's life without losing my sense of human dignity. And I kept my word. But up to the last day I found it was necessary to renew the struggle every day to keep that sense, because the conditions of life never ceased to undermine it and to encourage a state of subhuman apathy." (30 L)

In letter after letter she tried to communicate this overwhelmingly dehumanizing effect of factory life to Bernard, but without great success. "If I, who am vaguely supposed to have learned to express myself, cannot make myself understood by you, in spite of your goodwill," she wrote him, "one asks oneself how any understanding will ever be reached between the average worker and employer." (44 L)

Finally, her advocacy of the workers' cause both when convenient and inconvenient led to a break between her and Bernard. The event which triggered the rupture of their relations was the massive wave of sit-in strikes that spread through France in May and June 1936. The immediate cause of the strikes was the victory of the Popular Front (a coalition of liberal, socialist, communist, and other leftist parties) in the April–May elections. For the first time since the establishment of the Third Republic in 1871, a genuinely socialist government was elected, and the workers were lifted up with the hope that their day had finally come and that the Popular Front government would put through long-overdue reforms. So profound was the relief and sense of hope that workers all over France began spontaneously to go on sit-down strikes and occupy the factories; by June 3 almost a million workers were on strike and the economy was virtually paralyzed.

Simone Weil, who went to Paris early in June and visited the Renault plant where she had worked, interpreted the precipitousness of the strikes as the effect of suffering too long endured. "All who have suffered," she wrote in an article on the strikes that appeared in *La Révolution Prolétarienne* on June 10, "know that when one believes that one is going to be delivered of an unbearably long and painful suffering, the last days of waiting are intolerable." (230 CO)

Despite the workers' impatience, the strikes were conducted peacefully; indeed, as Weil described them, at least initially they were joyful. The workers brought in their wives and families, sang and chatted and played cards, and generally made themselves at home in their work places, where they had never been allowed to feel at home before. Weil was elated over the strikes not because she expected revolutionary consequences from them—if anything, she was rather pessimistic in regard to the long-range results of the strikes—but because, at least for a short period of time, the workers had dared to "hold up their heads . . . to feel themselves men." (230 CO)

When she had occasion to write to Bernard on June 10 to cancel an appointment with him because she had to go to Paris, she chose, in the interests of honesty, not to disguise what she felt. She acknowledged that the strikes brought her "feelings of unspeakable joy and relief." Whatever consequences the strikes might have, she wrote, "nothing can destroy the value of these lovely days of joy and fraternity." (52 L) Bernard, however, was mortally offended that she would express such feelings to him, reading them as the crowing of the victor over the vanquished employers. He terminated their correspondence with a stiff note.

Weil's support of the striking workers was much more complex and much less uncritical than Bernard gave her credit for. As soon as it appeared that the workers had made their power felt, she immediately began to stress the need for worker, as well as employer, responsibility: " Since you intend to compel industrial enterprises to acknowledge the force of your claims," she wrote in a sort of sample address to hypothetical workers, "you must be able to face the responsibilities of the new situation which you have brought about." (60 L) After the completion of the negotiations that gave the workers the right to collective bargaining, a forty-hour week, a seven to fifteen percent wage increase, two weeks' paid vacation, and an end to reprisals against them for joining unions, she published an open letter to one of the four million unskilled workers who then came into the trade unions, reminding the new union member that now that he had new rights, he also had new responsibilities: "When you had no rights, you recognized no obligations. Now you are somebody, you have strength, you have received some advantages; but in return you have acquired some responsibilities. . . . Now you must work to make yourself capable of assuming them; otherwise these newly-acquired advantages will vanish one fine day like a dream. One preserves his rights only if he is capable of exercising them properly." (244 CO)

Once the break with Bernard eliminated the possibility that she would ever be able to work at Rosières, Weil turned again to her first employer, Auguste Detoeuf, and spoke with him of her "project of returning to your factory as a worker for an indefinite period, in order to collaborate with you . . . on some attempted reforms." (245 CO; cf. 55 L) Whether she was thinking of undertaking such a project immediately or merely had it in mind for some unspecified future date is not certain; in any event, before she could pursue it further, the Spanish Civil War erupted.

* * *

Spain, like France, had a Popular Front government, and, as in France, the emergence of the Popular Front* had heightened long-standing and violent hostility between the left and the right. In France the polarization between the two groups was such that in the eyes of the right, socialism was increasingly identified with communism, political choice seemed to be narrowed to the

---

*The Popular Front was formed after Russia recognized in 1934 that Nazi Germany was a threat to its own security and began to reverse the international communist policy of noncooperation with other leftist parties. Word went out from Moscow, first via *Pravda* in May 1934 and then via the Seventh Congress of the Communist International in the summer of 1935, that the European communist parties should unite with the other parties of the left in a common effort to resist fascism.[6]

two extremes of communism and fascism, and some people were saying, "Better Hitler than [Socialist Prime Minister] Blum." In Spain the polarization was even more intense, the mutual hatred of left and right deeper, and the threat of revolution and counterrevolution more real. Uprisings, strikes, arson, murder, and general violence and disorder were widespread. The inability of the Popular Front government to maintain order provided the excuse for the rightist military insurrection launched by Generals Mola and Franco on July 17.[7] But if the generals had expected an easy victory because of the weakness of the Republican government, they miscalculated the strength of the revolutionary passions of the people, and they precipitated not only a civil war but a revolution. What ensued was nominally a war between the nationalist rebels and the legitimate Republican government, but in actuality the conduct of the Republican side of the war was shared, if not dominated, by the revolutionary forces of the left, the anarchist, anarcho-syndicalist, socialist, and communist organizations and their militias.[8]

Simone Weil had rejoiced over the French strikes of June 1936, but the civil war in Spain stirred her to action. For all her sympathy for the French strikers, her feeling was that the workers' movement in France was heading in the undesirable direction of state socialism; for this reason she had done nothing "to promote or prolong the strikes," and she did not expect revolutionary changes to follow from them. In Spain, however, she saw quite another phenomenon, and her moral commitment to the social transformation for which the Spanish workers and peasants were fighting was so intense that she could not bear to remain away from the front lines.

As she wrote later about her decision to go to Spain, she did not like war, and until 1939 she resolutely condemned international wars because, whatever their goals, the means employed in carrying on a war between states always tended to strengthen the power of the state at the expense of the people. "War is inconceivable," she wrote in 1933, "without an oppressive organization, without a system in which one group, which gives orders, has absolute power over those who carry out orders." (241 EHP) She also recognized that to the degree a revolution turned into a war, it bred the very structures of oppression it was fighting to overthrow: "war, even made by revolutionaries in order to defend the revolution which they have made, constitutes a counterrevolutionary factor." (241 EHP) In another essay of the same year (1933) she put it more succinctly: "Revolutionary war is the tomb of the revolution and will remain so as long as the soldiers themselves, or rather the armed citizens, are not given the means of making war without being subject to an oppressive military apparatus." (236–37 EHP) Her enthusiasm for the Spanish Civil War stemmed from the fact that anarchism* and anarcho-syndicalism were stronger and more widespread among the workers and peasants in Spain than in any other European country, and there seemed to be grounds for a real hope that a people's revolution which would replace the state with a system of "self-contained and self-governing communes"[9] was truly in the making. As historian James Joll put it, "for a brief period in the summer of 1936 the anarchist revolution seemed about to be achieved."[10]

Like many others of the left, Simone Weil saw in Spain the same idealistic revolutionary spirit that had flared briefly at the time of the French Revolution, the Commune of 1871, and the Russian Revolution. "This

---

*Despite the popular stereotype of anarchists as terrorists, there is a branch of anarchist thought which is idealistic, egalitarian, and concerned with human dignity, and which values both individualism and cooperation. There is considerable similarity between Simone Weil's social/political thought in the mid-1930s and that of the more idealistic and less violent strains of anarchism.

is indeed the Revolution," she wrote exultantly upon her arrival in Barcelona early in August. It seemed to her that she was actually living through one of "those historic periods—1792, 1871, 1917—which one reads books about. . . . one of those extraordinary periods, which until now have not lasted, when those who have always obeyed assume responsibility." (209 EHP) Even though Barcelona seemed unchanged from the days of peace and it was difficult to believe that it was the capital of a region *en plein guerre civile*, she observed that one thing was really changed: "The power is to the people. The men in blue [i.e., the workers] command."

Once in Barcelona, she went first to the headquarters of the POUM (Partido Obrero de Unificación Marxista), an anti-Stalinist and extremely revolutionary dissident communist group whose founder, Joaquin Maurín, was the brother-in-law of her friend Boris Souvarine. Maurín had been in Galicia giving lectures when the war broke out and had disappeared soon after Galicia had been overwhelmed by nationalist forces. She volunteered to go into Galicia either to find him or to find out what had happened to him, but her offer was refused on the grounds that what she was proposing was too dangerous and had too little chance of success.[11]

Although concern for her friend's brother-in-law took her first to the POUM, Weil's strongest sympathies lay with the Spanish anarcho-syndicalist groups, of which the CNT (Confederación Nacional de Trabajo) was the largest. (The CNT was for all practical purposes in charge of the war in the Catalonia-Aragon region.) She was well aware at the time she went to Spain that the CNT and the more ideologically oriented FAI (Federación Anarquista Ibérica) were a mixed bag in which "immorality, cynicism, fanaticism, and cruelty rubbed elbows with one another," but she also saw in the anarchist organizations "love and the spirit of brotherhood and . . . that concern for honor which is so beautiful in the humiliated." What she saw and heard after several weeks in Spain badly disillusioned her, but at the outset it seemed to her that "those who came to the anarchist movement animated by an ideal outweighed those impelled by a taste for violence and disorder." (221 EHP; cf. 106 L)

From Barcelona she wrote to her parents that journalists (she had gotten into Spain with journalist's credentials) and "generally speaking foreigners" were not allowed to go to the front because "they are an encumbrance."[12] However, after a few days she left Barcelona and made her way through the province of Lérida into the Aragon region and to the town of Pina on the Ebro River, about two hundred forty kilometers west of Barcelona. The front was between Pina and the city of Saragossa, about fifteen kilometers farther west on the Ebro. Buenaventura Durruti, one of the most famous, dedicated, and violent of the anarchist leaders, was in charge of a column of troops in the area and was planning an assault to recapture Saragossa from the nationalists.

On Friday and Saturday, August 14 and 15, Weil recorded in her *Journal d'Espagne*[13] some notes on her conversations with peasants in Pina. She asked them if they were in agreement about farming collectively (one of the primary goals of the left was the expropriation of large estates and redistribution of land to the peasants to be worked individually or collectively, "according to their own decision"[14]). They affirmed (though not very categorically, she noted) that they preferred to work collectively rather than separately. She asked them how they lived; she was told that they worked day and night and ate badly. Most of them did not know how to read. She asked other questions about their lives and opinions, and one can sense her testing the ideas she had formed of the situation in Spain against the reality. Although she apparently regarded her journalist's credentials only as a means of getting into Spain, it is clear that she wanted to observe and to learn as well as to fight, and her *Journal d'Espagne* is a brief testament of such observation. She noted the sharp feeling of inferiority among the peasants, a feeling which the revolutionary situation had not changed. Despite the anarchist ideal of complete egalitarianism, she found that differences in power had their effect on the relations between the militiamen and the peasants. In her later reflections on the war Weil wrote, "an abyss separated the armed militiamen from the unarmed population, an abyss exactly like that which separates the rich and the poor." (224 EHP; cf. 109 L)

Among the CNT militias in Pina she found a small international group composed of about twenty Italians, Bulgarians, Germans, Spaniards, and Frenchmen, two of whom she knew.[15] She asked to be allowed to join the group and was accepted. On Monday, August 17, she was in the Pina school where her group was installed; just as she was writing Boris Souvarine that she had not yet heard a shot fired, "BOOM!"—a bomb fell nearby. With everyone else she grabbed her rifle and dashed outside into the cornfield, where she lay on her back in the mud in order to shoot at the planes. They flew on, out of range. She observed with interest her own psychological response to being in a situation of real risk; she noted, after inspecting the crater left by this first small bomb, that she had not felt fear at all. Later that same afternoon some of her group crossed the river in order to search for and burn some enemy corpses; having accomplished that task, when they were heading back toward the river, someone spotted a house. It was decided that some of them would approach the house. Suddenly, realizing that her comrades were making a raid on the house, Weil felt the stirrings of fear. She did not know what usefulness there could be in such a move, and she knew that if any of them were captured, they would be shot.

Two days later, on another and more risky expedition across the river, she again noted the psychological and perceptual experiences that accompanied uncertainty and danger. Most of the group had gone off on a mission, leaving her in the bivouac with the German cook. Nationalist troops were in the area, and being left in camp was almost as dangerous as going on the mission. While they waited for the others to return, she noticed her German comrade's visible nervousness. She was not nervous, she decided—"but," she observed, "how intensely everything around me exists! War without prisoners. If one is captured, one is shot." Later, nationalist planes flew over making aerial reconnaisance; everyone took cover. She lay on her back in a trench under a tree and looked at "the leaves, the blue sky. A very beautiful day. If they capture me, they will kill me.... But it is deserved. Our troops have spilled a lot of blood. I am morally an accomplice." (214 EHP)

The expedition across the river was expected to last several days, and a camp kitchen, carefully camouflaged to prevent it being spotted by nationalist reconnaisance, was set up. A hole was dug for the cooking fire so that when a pot or pan was placed over it at ground level, the coals beneath were not visible. The camouflage was only too successful. Early in the morning of August 20, Simone Weil walked through the kitchen area. Over the hidden fire the cook had placed a large pan filled with boiling oil, probably to fry *churros*, a kind of breakfast fritter. She did not see the inconspicuous frying pan and put her left foot squarely in the center of it. Her shoe protected the bottom of her foot, but the oil splashed up around her instep and ankle, and she suffered second- and third-degree burns. She was forced to return to Barcelona. There she was found by her parents, who, anxious about her safety, had entered Spain illegally to look for her. They had her hospitalized in Sitgés, near Barcelona, and then, dissatisfied with the treatment she was receiving in the hospital, took her to their pension in Sitgés and nursed her themselves.

Weil made no entries in her *Journal d'Espagne* for two weeks. The entries resume on September 5 with brief accounts, for the most part without comment, of actions perpetrated by the anarchists which she could only have regarded as betrayals of the anarchist ideals and of the revolution. She reports a punitive expedition by the Sitgés militia to kill ten local "fascists" (a very broad term, too often used to cover anyone who had not joined a leftist militia) after ten of the militiamen had been killed in a raid on Majorca. In Lérida the column of García Oliver, acting against orders by the CNT, burned the cathedral and broke into a prison, where they massacred twenty prisoners. In Villafranca, near Sitgés, the priest and the large landholders, who simply because of their positions were regarded as fascists, were executed. The ideals of responsibility, of respect for all human beings, of social and political equality—all the values for which, in the beginning, Simone Weil had believed the war was being fought—were swallowed up in the license bred by war: "As soon as men know that they can kill without fear of punishment or blame," she wrote in 1938, looking back on Spain, "they kill; or at least they encourage killers with approving smiles. . . . The very purpose of the whole struggle is soon lost in an atmosphere of this sort. For the purpose can only be defined in terms of the public good, of the welfare of men—and men have become valueless." (108 L)

She left Spain on September 22, primarily at the urging of her parents. Back in Paris, she continued her dispassionate observations of the interior developments of the Republican side. They were not happy develop-ments, and they bore out all too well the analysis of the course of revolutionary wars she had made in 1933. Dur-ing the autumn of 1936 the people's war gave way to a war conducted along traditional military lines, with "a single Republican command, obligatory military service, discipline, and a 'unified war industry.'"[16] In an unpublished essay probably written in October or November 1936 Weil pointed out the similarities between the course of the civil war in Spain and that of the Russian Revolution. In Russia, she wrote, Lenin had publically demanded "a State in which there would be neither army, nor police, nor bureaucracy distinct from the population." But what emerged after a long civil war was the "heaviest bureaucratic, military and police machine which has ever weighed on an unfortunate people." Weil saw the same machinery of oppression emerging in Catalonia. Oppressive military and economic measures—conscription, the application of the old military code to the militias, production speed-up and extra hours of unpaid work in the factories—were being decreed by the Generalitat (the autonomous regional government of Catalonia) in which "some of our FAI comrades have leading positions." The necessities of civil war, she concluded, and the atmosphere generated by it "outweigh the aspirations which one seeks to defend by means of civil war." (218 EHP)

If the necessities of war were such that the development of the internal machinery of oppression was an unavoidable outcome even of a civil war fought for the most libertarian ideals, all the more, she reasoned, must an increase in the machinery of oppression be the outcome of international wars. She argued, therefore, that every effort must be made to avoid war between nations. She sharply criticized Leon Blum because of the inconsistency between his noninterventionist position on Spain and his support of the principle of collective security—collective security being, in effect, an attempt to preserve peace by, if necessary, making war. In not intervening in Spain, the French were, in her eyes, sacrificing the Spanish people in order to avoid European war; Weil had agreed to the necessity of that sacrifice, but she found it unjustifiable for France to subsequently risk war by intervening in some other European conflict, even to protect its own colonies or to defend nations with whom it had treaties of military alliance. In the name of peace, she wrote angrily, France had decided that "we will not make war to prevent the Spanish workers and peasants from being exterminated by a clique of savages more or less decorated with military gold braid. But, should the occasion arise, we will make war for Alsace-Lorraine, for Morocco, for Russia, for Czechoslovakia, and, if some Tardieu had signed a treaty of alliance with Honolulu, we would make war for Honolulu." (253 EHP)

Through the end of 1936 and the beginning of 1937 Simone Weil's outlook on the future grew increasingly grim. Even though French foreign policy was designed to avoid war if at all possible, France was rearming and defense industries were being nationalized. In terms of what it did to unite the military and industrial bureaucracies as well as to increase the power of the state over the economy as a whole, Weil thought that preparation for war was the next worst thing to war itself. And given the direction taken by events in France and the tensions in Europe in 1937, she thought that military preparations would come more and more "to dominate all the everyday aspects of existence." She viewed the the final outcome of this trend with extreme pessimism. "Capitalism will be destroyed," she wrote, "but not by the working class. It will be destroyed by the development of national defense in each country, and replaced by the totalitarian state. That," she concluded bitterly, "is the revolution we shall have."[17]

5

1937–1939

Because of the burns she had suffered in Spain, Simone Weil had been unable to return to teaching in the fall of 1936, and she had applied for a medical leave of absence for the autumn trimester. Her injury was slow to heal, her headaches were increasingly frequent and severe, and she applied for extensions of leave in December and again in March. In March and April she spent six weeks at a hospital in Switzerland undergoing treatment for her headaches; she was not cured, but she was rested and refreshed, and after her release from the hospital she went on by herself to Milan, Rome, Florence, and Assisi, where she immersed herself in museums, concerts, Gregorian chant at St. Peter's on Pentecost, and the beauties of the Italian countryside.

The trip to Italy was a luminous episode in what was otherwise a painful time both in terms of her own physical health and in terms of what was happening in the world. She was unwell and unable to work in the summer after her return from Italy, and though she accepted a teaching job at St.–Quentin for the autumn trimester of 1937, she was forced to apply for another medical leave in January because of headaches and extreme fatigue. The enthusiasm generated by the strikes of 1936, the election of the Popular Front, and the first months of the war in Spain was gone. Bilbao fell to the nationalists in Spain in June; France was on the verge of bankruptcy, and the Popular Front was dying. Fascism was expanding; Italy had invaded Ethiopia the year before; in defiance of the Versailles treaty, Hitler had militarized the west bank of the Rhine and was soon to annex Austria.

Reflecting on the state of the world in 1937, Weil increasingly saw the need for a new framework in which to try to understand social phenomena which Marxism was inadequate to explain: war and oppression. "Marxists have never analysed the phenomenon of war," she wrote, "nor its relation to the economic system; for I do not call the simple assertion that capitalist greed is the cause of wars an analysis." (151 OL) Nor, she thought, did the Marxist idea that economics is the determining factor in all social relationships fully account for the total submissiveness of the oppressed: "When an old working man, unemployed and left to starve, dies quietly in the street or some slum, the submission which extends to the very point of death cannot be explained by the play of vital necessities." (142 OL) And there was no economic explanation—or any explanation at all, Weil thought—for the fact that one man could effectively hold the lives of millions in his hands: "Is there," she asked, "at the present time, over the whole of the earth's surface, a single mind which can conceive even vaguely how it is that one man in the Kremlin has the power to cause any head whatever to fall within the confines of the Russian frontiers?" (141 OL)

Economics, she concluded, could not provide "the key to social riddle." She began, tentatively, to talk about the mechanics of social organization in terms of the Heraclitean idea of the unceasing struggle of opposing forces and the ever-shifting equilibrium between them. "Every social *status quo*," she wrote early in 1937, "rests upon an equilibrium of forces or pressures, similar to the equilibrium of fluids"; (169 SE) these forces are expressed in social terms as tendencies toward order and toward the conservation of the status quo, on the one hand, and tendencies toward change on the other. The problem facing Europe, she ventured, is that the perpetual nature of the conflict between opposing social forces is not understood. She saw at the root of this problem an intellectual failure, the same overdevelopment of abstraction, the same separation of the mind from its object, the world, for which she criticized modern mathematics. "The mathematician," she had written in her first Notebook, "lives in a universe apart, where objects are signs. The relation between sign and thing signified no longer exists; the play of interchange between signs develops of itself and for itself." (31 FLN) The consequences of this separation of thought from the world were "intellectual decadence" and the loss of "the very elements of intelligence: the ideas of limit, measure, degree, proportion, relation, comparison, contingency, interdependence, interrelation of means and ends." (156 SE)

In politics, the relationship between the sign and the thing signified having been lost sight of, words in the social and political vocabulary—"nation, security, capitalism, communism, fascism, order, authority, property, democracy"—become abstractions, "myths and monsters" for which men blindly fight and kill: "When empty words are given capital letters, then, on the slightest pretext, men will begin shedding blood for them and piling up ruin in their name." (156 SE) The place to start on the problems facing Europe, Weil suggested, is first of all the sphere of thought: "To clarify thought, to discredit the intrinsically meaningless words, and to define the use of others by precise analysis—to do this, strange though it may appear, might be a way of saving human lives." (156 SE)

The year 1937 marked the nadir of Weil's disillusionment with all varieties of current social thought. Neither the revolutionaries nor the defenders of the status quo, she charged, knew what they were doing, and neither revolutionaries nor capitalists had developed an adequate framework in which to understand the workings of social phenomena. Her own attempts to do so led her to see a radical opposition between thought and the forces governing society. In the brief "Meditation on Obedience and Liberty," written in the second half of 1937, Weil attempted to analyze the nature of the social force which made oppression possible. How, she asked herself, was it possible for a small number of people to oppress multitudes? "That a number of men should submit themselves to a single man [she was thinking of Stalin] through fear of being killed by him is astonishing enough," she wrote. "But what are we to make of it when they remain submissive to him to the point of dying at his orders? When there are at least as many risks attached to obedience as there are to rebellion, how is obedience maintained?" (141 OL) It was maintained, she concluded, by the inculcation of a feeling of inferiority in those who obey: "The man who obeys, whose movements, pains, pleasures are determined by the word of another, feels himself to be inferior, not by accident, but by nature. . . . It seems to those who obey that some mysterious inferiority has predestined them to obey from all eternity, and every mark of scorn—even the tiniest—which they suffer at the hands of their superiors or their equals, every order they receive, and especially every act of submission they themselves perform confirms them in this feeling." (145 OL)

The functioning of any social order in which the few command and the many obey depends on the submission of those who obey, and the force which makes such an unequal situation possible depends on the maintenance of the falsehood that those at the bottom of the social scale are without value. Thus, Weil concluded, there was an absolute opposition between the social order and both truth and justice: "Everything that contributes toward giving those who are at the bottom of the social scale the feeling that they possess a value is to a certain extent subversive." She found a smilar opposition between the value-oriented human mind and the social order: "all that is highest in human life, every effort of thought, every effort of love, has a corrosive effect on the established order.... Insofar as [thought] is ceaselessly creating a scale of values 'that is not of this world,' it is the enemy of the forces which control society." (145 OL)

"Meditation on Obedience and Liberty" is the most pessimistic account of the relationship between the inspirations of the mind and heart and the forces of the social order that Simone Weil ever wrote. "Those who want to think, love, and transpose in all purity into political action what their mind and heart inspire them with ... can only perish murdered, forsaken even by their own people, vilified after their death by history, as happened to the Gracchi." The social order, she concludes, "though necessary, is essentially evil, whatever it may be." (146 OL) Attempts to mitigate that evil, to try to influence the "play of forces which control the movement of history," was, she thought, impossible "without contaminating oneself or incurring certain defeat."

Over the course of the next several years Weil began to distinguish between what she called *le social* (the social order, the social element) and "the social City." She used *le social* to refer to the social order as a purely material phenomenon, a "great beast" (to borrow Plato's image) whose conceptions of value are shaped by its animal likes and dislikes; the social City, on the other hand, she saw as something totally different. What distinguished the social City was that it is "rooted" in "nature, the past, tradition" (296–7 N); the City was for her a manifestation of justice and beauty incarnate in human relationships, a work of art created in a human medium (in *Venise sauvée*, the verse drama she was to begin in 1940, Venice exemplifies the social City). She began to develop this idea of rootedness—which was to become an increasingly powerful metaphor for her in the last years of her life—in the late 1930s. The idea of rootedness, and all that it implied for her, provided a counterbalance to her despairing assessment of the futility of political action in 1937, an assessment which was indeed based on observations of phenomena she would later specify as symptomatic of extreme spiritual and cultural uprootedness.

In letters written in 1939 Weil began to talk about social milieus which "permit the existence of an atmosphere in which spiritual values (for lack of a better term) can develop." (109 EHP; cf. 79 SE) These milieus "favorable to the development of the soul" could only exist, she thought, in situations in which power was not a dominant value; they could be destroyed both by internal factors—the growth of a "strong, systematic, centralized power"— and by external ones such as military conquest and, especially, colonial conquest. Spiritual values, she recognized, were incarnate in individuals and environments and, like them, were vulnerable. "Why does everyone go on repeating that commonplace about the impossibility of spiritual values being destroyed by brute force?" she asked in a letter in the spring of 1939. "It destroys them very quickly and very easily." (79 SE) In an essay of the same period Weil continued in the same vein: "contrary to what is often said, spiritual values are very easily destroyed by force, even to the complete obliteration of all trace of them. Indeed," she went on, "if this were not so, why should anyone except the meanest self-seekers [*les âmes basses*] be much concerned about politics?" (191 SE)

Simone Weil's increasing concern with spiritual values in the late 1930s and particularly the specifically Christian assumptions that begin to appear in her writing in 1939 indicate that a significant change took place in her thinking during this period. It was not something in the nature of a *bouleversement*, a complete turning upside down of her life and values. On the contrary; she was, as she points out in her "Spiritual Autobiography," brought up in a culture which, however secularized, still regarded the Christian values as ideals, and she felt herself culturally if not religiously born into Christianity. Both by temperament and by early philosophical training she was oriented toward the realm of value, and she herself did not consider that there was much difference between a person of her philosophical orientation and a theist. There was no real difference, she told her philosophy students in 1934, between the person who believes in God and the person who believes only in the human spirit, as long as one "doesn't allow the superstition of miracles to come in." (112 LP) Nevertheless, there is a difference, and an important one, in her writings after 1937–38; not a radical difference in the sense of change in the very roots and beginnings of her thought (those remain essentially the same) but a change (to continue the metaphor) in the upper part of the tree—she unfolds, she blossoms, she puts forth surprising leaves. Her vision expands; she begins to try to see all of Western culture, from the ancient Greeks to the present, in terms of a large and all-embracing whole; and she sees everything—to use one of her favorite images—in a new light.

Prior to 1937–38, the limits of her vision of the world were the limits of rational consciousness. According to William James, who discovered in his own nitrous oxide experience the existence of other realms of the mind, "our normal waking consciousness, rational consciousnes as we call it, is but one special type of consciousness, whilst all about it, parted from it by the filmiest of screens, there lie potential forms of consciousness entirely different. We may go through life without suspecting their existence; but apply the requisite stimulus, and at a touch they are there in all their completeness. . . ."[1] Simone Weil inadvertently—for she was certainly not consciously seeking any such thing—triggered the "requisite stimulus" of which James speaks when she was in Assisi in the spring of 1937. She was in many respects very well prepared. Her intellectual training had developed very highly her capacity for sustained attention, and she brought this capacity to her contemplation of works of art; she was in the habit of focusing her attention, literally for hours, on a work of art which she found extremely beautiful. She wrote to a friend that she had spent "an hour or two" (75 L) contemplating the fresco of the Last Supper when she was in Milan, and she refers in her *Notebooks* to "three hours spent before a fresco of Giotto's." (27 N) When she was in Assisi, she visited the little Franciscan chapel of Santa Maria degli Angeli, which she thought an "incomparable marvel of purity." (67 WG) Alone in the chapel, she became absorbed in its beauty. The focus of her attention must have been more intense than ever before, for she went beyond the level of aesthetic contemplation and found herself in another dimension of consciousness; she felt, she wrote later, in the presence of "something stronger than I was" which "compelled me for the first time in my life to go down on my knees." (67–8 WG)

A recent writer on the brain/mind relationship describes what may happen in such experiences:

Meditational trance seems to represent a massive inhibition of almost all cortical systems. . . . sensory perceptual and cognitive mechanisms are brought to a stop, and the sense of ego dissolved.... As St. John of the Cross observed, the soul must strip itself of all forms and manners of knowledge.... Time and space sense also goes. When all the functions performed by the brain as we understand it have been stilled, what remains? Not, as one might suppose, nothing at all, but an amazing sense of deity, to which mystics of all ages bear witness.[2]

"*Momentary non-operation of the mind*," Simone Weil later wrote in a fragmentary entry in her *Notebooks*, "*...insertion of eternity into time*." (96 N)

In the spring of 1938 she had another experience, somewhat similar to the one in Assisi and also triggered by an unusually intense effort of concentration on beauty. With her mother, who shared her love of music, she spent Holy Week at the Benedictine abbey at Solesmes, which is famous for its Gregorian chant. She attended all the offices in spite of the fact that she was suffering from splitting headaches and "each sound hurt me like a blow." Describing later what happened, she wrote that an "extreme effort of attention made it possible for me to get outside of this miserable flesh, to leave it to suffer alone heaped up in a corner, and to find a pure and perfect joy in the extraordinary beauty of the chant and the words." (43 AD; cf. 68 WG)

Finally, late in 1938, in similar circumstances of pain and intense concentration on something beautiful— in this case the poem "Love" by the English metaphysical poet George Herbert—the generalized sense of deity she felt in Assisi became particularized for her as Christ. At the culminating point of a violent headache, when she was concentrating most intensely in order to endure the pain, the dialogue in the poem between the soul and Love (a figure of Christ) became an experiential reality for her. She felt, she wrote later, "the presence of a love" (69 WG) that was "more personal, more certain, more real than that of a human being." (140 L) It was "Christ[3] himself," she wrote, and he "came down and took possession of me."

Her later reflections on this experience and similar ones subsequent to it gave Weil the material to develop a mystical theology and also added another level to her understanding of philosophy, science, art, and culture as a whole. In the light of her own mystical experience, she came to see Plato, whom she had always loved, as a mystic; using an image she would frequently employ when describing the relation of the supernatural to this world, she began to speak of the *Iliad* as "bathed in Christian light." (70 WG) And she now began to see in the different religious traditions of antiquity different expressions of "one and the same" essence (502 N) so that she could say that "Dionysus and Osiris are in a certain sense Christ himself." (70 WG) Perhaps most important, from the point of view of the whole of her thinking, her new perspective gave another dimension to her vision of a truly humane civilization. She now began to envision—and to look for historical evidence of—a civilization which had at its core an apprehension of mystical truth. And she began to see the enormous crises of her own times as the ultimate result of the loss of this core of truth.

*   *   *

By the spring of 1939 Simone Weil's long-held antiwar position began to be severely eroded by her growing awareness of the scope of Hitler's ambitions and a premonition of the unimaginable destruction of human values that would result if Hitlerism were not resisted. In "*Réflexions en vue d'une bilan*" (English title, "Cold War Policy in 1939," probably written in April or May of that year) she drew up a balance sheet between the terrible human cost of war and the likely costs of German hegemony in Europe without war and concluded, for the last time, that the cost of war was greater. She advocated a foreign policy designed to resist German expansionism as much as possible without provoking violence, in the hope that the dynamism of Nazism might "run its whole course to success and then to collapse without any war." (190 SE) It was a policy of the lesser evil; she did not think that German hegemony would be anything but bad, but she was certain that a world war would be worse. However, some time in May her position shifted; she wrote later that "after a very painful inner struggle" she had decided that, in spite of her pacifist inclinations, there was "an overriding obligation . . . to work for Hitler's destruction." (158 L)

What changed her mind was a reassessment of European feeling in regard to the real danger of Hitler achieving not merely German hegemony but "universal domination" comparable to that of Imperial Rome. Two factors, she felt, were necessary for Hitler to realize his vision of the Third Reich as the successor of the Roman Empire: first his own belief that he could actually do so, and second the belief in all the other countries of Europe that it was really possible that he could do so. Some time in the late spring of 1939 she felt the climate of European opinion shift, and at that point she abandoned her pacifism. The possibility of German hegemony was one thing; the possibility of German regarding Europe as colonies to be enslaved and exploited was quite another. "The loss to humanity," she wrote, "would be beyond all computation." (191 SE)

Since the seizure of Czechoslovakia Simone Weil had been comparing Hitler's methods of expansion with the methods of conquest employed by Rome and had found many similarities. In a lengthy essay called "*Quelques réflexions sur les origines de l'Hitlerism*" (English title, "The Great Beast"), written after the outbreak of the war in the autumn of 1939, she analyzed in detail the Roman methods of imposing domination, finding in them a policy of "cold, calculated, systematic cruelty, never mitigated by change of humour, prudence, shame, or pity—cruelty that can neither be stayed by courage, dignity, or force, nor mollified by submission, supplication, and tears." (106 SE) In the skill displayed by the Romans in subduing the world Weil saw intelligence put entirely to the service of domination; it made them invincible and comfortable and convinced that they were always in the right, but it deprived them of all spiritual life:

In a general way, the Romans enjoyed that tough, unshakeable, impenetrable collective self-satisfaction which makes it possible to commit crimes with a perfectly untroubled conscience. When conscience is impermeable by truth there must be a degradation of heart and mind which obscures and weakens thought; and that is why the only Roman contribution to the history of science is the murder of Archimedes. In compensation, however, this complete self-satisfaction, reinforced by power and conquest, is contagious, and we are still under its influence today. (116 SE)

Rome's domination of the Mediterranean world, Simone Weil argued, brought not civilization but centuries of spiritual barrenness. "It would be singular," she wrote, "if civilization could be exported from one country to another" by methods of domination that were essentially calculated to paralyze the minds of the conquered. What Rome actually produced—an extremely effective system of administration, roads, bridges, and improvements in material well-being—was not, in Weil's opinion, civilization. To her, civilization was the fruit of those "human milieus" in which constraint—and especially constraint imposed by fear—was at a minimum, in which obedience was freely given rather than imposed by force, and in which social conditions allowed the "development of the soul."

This conception of civilization implies a fundamental hierarchy, which Simone Weil takes for granted, of the spirit over the material world, the mind over the body, and what she would later call the supernatural part of the soul over the natural or psychological part of the soul. In the natural world, at least vis-à-vis the human being, this hierarchy is inverted; the forces of nature "infinitely surpass" the human being, and he is inevitably subject to suffering and death. It was the task of the human being, she believed, to create a balance between the mind and the world by his grasp of the relationships in nature, to bring humanity and the natural world into an equilibrium such that, insofar as possible, neither is destroyed by the other. Similarly, she saw it as the task of the human spirit to achieve an equilibrium between the individual and society—and it is society which, now that human beings have mastered nature to a hitherto undreamed-of degree, has replaced nature as an oppressive force. In her writings of this period Weil expresses more and more insistently the idea that the submission of the mind to force—and especially to force wielded by a human mind—is experienced as evil, causing not only physical suffering but spiritual suffering and even spiritual destruction. She recognized more and more clearly that there is an irremediable amount of evil in the world—we suffer and die— but she also felt, and insisted upon, an inescapable human obligation to reduce as much as possible the domination of one human being by another. To be fully human—to be humane—in her eyes was to refuse to either respect or practice domination; those who practiced or celebrated domination, like the Romans and their successors, were in her opinion inhuman, intellectually subservient to the very force they wielded and therefore, in spite of their position of dominance, base in soul.

As she saw Hitler's whole project of domination in Europe as analogous in policy and methods to Roman domination, she saw the resistance of the democratic countries to Hitler as part of the perennial struggle between what she called the Greek spirit and the Roman spirit. The Greeks had a conception of virtue and an understanding of the nature of force which she found unsurpassed; they knew the tragic inevitability of human subjection to force, but instead of glorifying only those

who wielded it triumphantly, they celebrated as their
heroes those who suffered under it without becoming base
themselves. (Weil used Sophocles's Antigone as a favorite example—Antigone who is condemned to death
for obeying the dictates of a higher law than those op-
erating in the world of force.) She saw the present war,
however, not simply as a struggle between the Germans
and the French, between a totalitarian state and the de-
mocracies, but between the Greek spirit and the Roman
spirit within France and democratic Europe. Although
France, she wrote, "has had many minds of the first order
which have been neither servants nor worshippers of
force," from the time of Louis XIV onward "the cult of
grandeur, conceived after the Roman model. . . . has been
handed down by an almost unbroken line of famous writers." Furthermore, the whole political structure of the
modern centralized bureaucratic state resembled, much
too closely for Weil's taste, "the political structure evolved
by Rome." Within the democratic states, thus, the problem was both spiritual and political: spiritual in terms of
the model of greatness held up for admiration, political
in terms of the existing state structures and the dynamisms
of power they set in motion. Both, she insisted, needed
to be changed for the sake of humanity and for the growth
of a human and humane civilization. Otherwise, even the
defeat of Germany would not solve the problem.

6

1939–1941

From the very beginning of World War II, Simone Weil wanted to be an active participant. When a student uprising in Prague was put down by the occupying Germans, she devised a project to parachute French arms and volunteers—including herself—into Czechoslovakia to help support a popular resistance movement. She presented her project to "a number of important political figures,"[1] but it was dismissed out of hand. She then thought of organizing a corps of nurses who would accompany soldiers on the front lines into battle in order to give emergency first aid to the wounded. Despite the risk to the nurses—and she of course intended to be one of them*—she argued that such a corps was justified because it would save the lives of men who would otherwise die from shock and loss of blood while waiting for stretcher bearers to arrive. Moreover, the element of risk was itself important. The example of a small group

*She took some first-aid training in Paris after the war broke out and also during her stay in New York.

of women willing to risk their lives in order to save the wounded and comfort the dying would have, she thought, a tremendous moral and symbolic value; it would represent a total commitment to the most humane ideals and would thus embody the French reply, as it were, to the special German units composed of men fanatically dedicated to the Nazi ideology. Such an example, Weil insisted, was necessary not only for its value in raising morale but in itself, as an active expression of the humanitarian values for which the French were fighting.

Weil heavily stressed the importance of moral factors in the war. France's claim to be defending liberty must, she insisted, be more than a matter of words, and the defeat of Germany, if it was to have any real meaning, must result from something more than French material superiority. A victory gained and held by force alone, as she had frequently argued during the preceding months, would mean only "the triumph in France of the traditions inherited from the Romans and Richelieu and Louis XIV and Napoleon. In other words, Hitler's system would not disappear; it would simply migrate, with all its characteristic aims and methods, to France." (139 SE) Moreover, Weil was not entirely sure that material superiority alone could conquer a Germany inflamed by the powerful mystique of National Socialism: "It may be that our victory depends upon the presence among us of a corresponding inspiration, but authentic and pure"—i.e., deriving from a love of truth and justice rather than from the worship of power. She felt that her proposed nurses' corps would be a living symbol of such a pure inspiration: "The mere persistence of a few humane services in the very centre of the battle, the climax of inhumanity, would be a signal defiance of the inhumanity which the enemy has chosen for himself and which he compels us also to practice." (150 L)

According to Simone Pétrement, no one seems to

have taken this project seriously. The elder Weils, who knew a member of the French Senate, asked him to receive their daughter and, "in order to calm her anxiety, her great need to participate in the war, to tell her that he would present her project" to the Senatorial Army Commission.[2] This was done, and nothing more was heard of the project. Simone Weil, however, believed that the senator's interest in her project was genuine, that it was received favorably by the commission, and that it was "well on the way" to being adopted by the Army, "but events [i.e., the beginning of the German offensive against France] moved too rapidly." (144 L)

Whether or not her project, if adopted, would have had the inspiriting effectiveness she hoped, there is no doubt that Weil was correct in her assessment of the part played by morale in war and of the weakness of the French in that quarter. The Germans had no quantitative material superiority over the French and British forces except in the matter of airplanes,[3] but when they launched their offensive against the West in the spring of 1940, they swept through Belgium in two days, made short work of the French defenses at Sedan near the Belgian border, and moved rapidly across France to the Channel, trapping the French and British divisions in the north and leaving Paris completely vulnerable to the German advance.[4]

In an attempt to save the situation, Premier Paul Reynaud called in the two most famous surviving generals of World War I, the aging Marshal Pétain and seventy-three-year-old General Weygand. Pétain, who had turned almost certain defeat into a crucial victory for the French at Verdun in 1916, was the symbol in the popular mind of dogged resistance to the enemy; Reynaud appointed him Minister of State and Vice-Premier. General Weygand, renowned as the "architect of the Allied victory"[5] in 1918, was made commander-in-chief of the army. Together, it was hoped, these two symbols of victorious France would pull together the disorganized and demoralized army and encourage the dispirited civilian population.

Simone Weil, following the movements of the armies with intense interest, would have liked nothing better than to have a hand in the reorganization of French strategy. "Do you know in whose place I would like to be?" she asked Simone Pétrement—to the latter's astonishment—at the time of Weygand's appointment. "I would like to be in Weygand's shoes."[6] The French high command could have used something like her white-hot fervor. Weygand, like Pétain, was at least half-convinced almost from the moment he accepted his new position that the war was as good as lost, and he had neither the will nor the ability to launch the swift, confident, and coordinated counteroffensive that would have been necessary to turn the tide of German success.[7] The downhill spiral of French defeat continued. Literally millions of refugees from the north fled south ahead of the advancing Germans; in the last weeks of May and early June, highways were clogged with cars, trucks, bicycles, and thousands on foot pushing wheelbarrows, carts, and baby carriages piled with their possessions. By the second week in June Parisians, too, were taking flight. The scene was both appalling and heartbreaking:

Paris, in June, 1940, was a city veiled in black. Thick clouds of soot from burning petrol dumps masked the blinding summer sky. Houses disgorged their contents into all kinds of vehicles; furniture, possessions and people were huddled under pyramids of mattresses. . . . Old people, piled into perambulators, were pushed along by weeping women, the children trailing after them, stupefied by the heat. . . . The authorities had left for Bordeaux, one after another the ministries were moving; the tradesmen were shutting up their shops. It was all over. There was already a sense of armistice about the abandonment of Paris. You hoped for an earthquake that you might escape the shame; you were glad of the pall of soot veiling the long lines of vehicles, four abreast, that suddenly blocked the great arteries leading to the south.[8]

Simone Weil had no intention of abandoning Paris. She was sure that the city would be defended, and she intended to stay and fight. Her parents, anxious for her safety, remained with her. On June 13, when the Germans were only a few miles outside of the city, the Weils left their apartment—according to Pétrement's account "to do some shopping"[9]—and found placards on the walls announcing that Paris would not be defended. Dismayed, Simone Weil was uncertain whether to go or stay.

Weil's uncertainty was met with her mother's determination to get her family to safety. Mme Weil prevailed, and they hurried to the train station. They found a crowd outside, prevented from entering by the guards. The last train, they learned, was full and about to leave. Mme Weil, having pushed her way through the crowd to the doors of the station, her husband and daughter in tow, insisted to the guard that her husband belonged on the train in his capacity as a doctor. After some argument the guard agreed to let Dr. Weil board the train, but the doctor refused to go unless his wife and daughter were allowed to accompany him. The guard gave in and admitted them to the station, and they squeezed aboard the train.[10] Only a few hours later—at 5 P.M. that evening—the Germans reached the outskirts of the city and demanded its surrender.

Almost immediately, Simone Weil began to regret her decision to leave. She wanted to get off at Montereau, about seventy-five kilometers southeast of Paris, but was dissuaded by the argument that the Germans advancing from the south and east would probably not be stopped before they reached the Loire. The Weils went on to Nevers, on the banks of the Loire, thinking that the French would try to hold the front to the east of the river. Nevers,

however, was not defended, and the city was occupied
by the Germans shortly after the Weils' arrival.

During the two weeks that the Weils were at Nevers
the French government was at Bordeaux, arguing whether
to go into exile and continue to conduct the war in conjunction with the British or to ask for an armistice and
make a separate peace. Although the continuation of the
war was, strictly speaking, a political rather than a military decision, Commander-in-Chief Weygand, backed
by Marshal Pétain, insisted that the government ask for
an armistice. Of all the military men involved, only young
General de Gaulle was still committed to keeping France
in the fight; when it was apparent that Premier Reynaud
was going to capitulate to the pressures for an armistice,
de Gaulle left for London and from there began to broad-
cast appeals for the formation of a French Resistance
movement. In Bordeaux, meanwhile, Reynaud resigned,
Marshal Pétain was named to succeed him, and on June
17 the Pétain government asked the Germans for an armistice. Although the terms were harsh and the Germans
made the circumstances of the signing as humiliating as
possible—it took place in the very railroad car in which
the victorious French had witnessed the signing of the
German armistice in 1918—most Frenchmen accepted
it with relief.

Under the terms of the armistice, France was divided
into two sectors, an occupied zone in the north covering
three-fifths of the country, including Paris and the entire
Atlantic coast, and a free zone in the south and southeast.
After the cessation of hostilities the Weils made their way
south from Nevers into the unoccupied zone. They stopped
first at Vichy, remaining there all of July and most of
August. Their sojourn in Vichy coincided with the period
during which the French Parliament relocated in Vichy,
voted to dissolve itself, and gave full legislative and ex-
ecutive powers to Marshal Pétain. During this time Si-

mone Weil was overcome with shame and fury at the
French capitulation and the willingness of the French
people as a whole to accept the armistice, which she
regarded as a "collective act of cowardice and treason."
(158 L) She was, as usual, outspoken, and her attitudes
were unpopular. According to Pétrement, some people
in Vichy avoided her, and others, who had admired her
before, "treated her with glacial coldness when she spoke
to them."[11] Psychologically she remained a combatant,
and she resolved to try to get to London and join the Free
French movement de Gaulle was trying to organize there.

In late August she and her parents went south to
Toulouse, apparently in hopes of leaving France via Spain.
After that proved fruitless, in mid-September they came
to Marseilles, where they remained until the spring of
1942. In her first months there Simone Weil made several
more unsuccessful attempts to get abroad. She also tried
to make contact with local resistance networks and evidently had some connection with at least two. She wrote
later that she had had "considerable responsibility for
distributing one of the most important clandestine pub-
lications in the free zone, *Les Cahiers de Témoignage
Chrétien*. (144 L) She also exerted herself to improve
conditions in a nearby internment camp for the Indochinese workers who had been brought to France to work
in defense factories and had made their way to Marseilles
in flight from the German occupation, and she did what
she could for several individuals—refugees from fascist
countries—who were interned in other camps for foreigners. Her books and papers were shipped from Paris,
and she continued her study of Greek thought, doing
numerous translations and contemplating a translation of
the whole of the *Iliad*. She took her long essay on the
Iliad, written in Paris the year before, to Jean Ballard,
editor of the *Cahiers du Sud*, the most important literary
magazine in the unoccupied zone. Ballard liked it, and
"The *Iliad*, or The Poem of Force" was published in the

Cahiers du Sud in the December 1940 and January 1941 issues.

The essay on the *Iliad* was written[12] shortly after the essay on the origins of Hitlerism and is in a way a companion piece to it. The essay on Hitlerism analyzes the methods and effects of domination from the point of view of a given political situation; "The *Iliad*, or The Poem of Force" is a meditation on force as a universal phenomenon to which all beings, by the very fact of being born, are subject. The *Iliad*, Weil writes in this essay, is "the purest and loveliest of mirrors" of the human condition, reflecting unflinchingly and compassionately the effects of force on the human spirit—effects which no one, either victor or victim, is spared: "Force is as pitiless to the man who possesses it, or thinks he does, as it is to its victims; the second it crushes, the first it intoxicates. The truth is, nobody really possesses it. The human race is not divided up, in the *Iliad*, into conquered persons, slaves, suppliants, on the one hand, and conquerors and chiefs on the other. In this poem there is not a single man who does not at one time or another have to bow his neck to force." (11 I) The nature of force is such that its "power of converting a man into a thing is a double one. . . . To the same degree, though in different fashions, those who use it and those who endure it are turned to stone." They are transformed "either to the level of inert matter, which is pure passivity, or to the level of blind force, which is pure momentum." (26 I) Nevertheless, the poet's compassion suffuses this panorama of violence: "Nothing precious is scorned, whether or not death is its destiny . . . no man is set above or below the condition common to all men; whatever is destroyed is regretted. . . . As for the warriors, victors or vanquished, those comparisons which liken them to beasts or things can inspire neither admiration nor contempt, but only regret that men are capable of being so transformed." (30, 32 I)

For Weil, the genius of both the Homeric epic and the tragedies of Aeschylus and Sophocles lay in the Greeks' perception of the ubiquitousness of human misery and in their compassionate attitude toward the spirit wounded by force. In Greek tragedy, she writes, "the shame of the coerced spirit is neither disguised, nor enveloped in facile pity, nor held up to scorn... more than one spirit bruised and degraded by misfortune is offered for our admiration." (34 I) This recognition of the inescapability of human misery, she insists, is a "pre-condition of justice and love." As long as a human being enjoying relatively good fortune believes that he is as separate from the unfortunate as he would be if the latter belonged to a totally distinct species—in other words, as long as he does not recognize misfortune as the common human lot from which no one is spared—he cannot "regard [the unfortunate] as fellow-creatures nor love [them] as he loves himself." (34 I) Such a recognition depends on a love of truth, which in practice entails a refusal to lie to oneself in order to protect oneself from the knowledge of one's own vulnerability. Only one who refuses to lie can perceive and portray misfortune fairly; and such portrayal is rare: "the tendency is either to treat the unfortunate person as though catastrophe were his natural vocation, or to ignore the effects of misfortune on the soul, to assume, that is, that the soul can suffer and remain unmarked by it, can fail, in fact, to be recast in misfortune's image." (35 I)

The compassionate vision reflected in Greek epic and tragedy found its "last marvelous expression," Weil thought, in the Gospels; thereafter, however, she saw it emerge only rarely—e.g., in the works of Villon, in Molière's *École des femmes*, Racine's *Phèdre*, Shakespeare's *Lear*—in the literature of the Christian West. The disappearance of the Greek vision from Western literature was, in her opinion, only too clearly related to the power orientation of the Roman Empire and the persistence of Roman values throughout subsequent centuries up to the present. She had argued in the essay on Hitlerism that a general recognition of the real implications of the Roman glorification of power, and a struggle against the seductions of power in all the European countries, are crucial to the political future of the West. In the conclusion to the essay on the *Iliad*, though she is speaking from a literary and cultural point of view, she says much the same thing: "Perhaps [the peoples of Europe] will yet rediscover the epic genius, when they learn that there is no refuge from fate, learn not to admire force, not to hate the enemy, not to scorn the unfortunate. How soon this will happen is another question." (37 I)

* * *

The worship of power implies a crisis of values. Behind the ascendency of fascism, behind the defeat of France, Simone Weil saw a moral failure,* a failure of values, ultimately a failure of thought (the French language suggests the intimate connection between thought and value in its word "*conscience*," which can mean both conscience in the moral sense and consciousness). "For a long time now," Weil wrote in the spring of 1941, "in every sphere without exception, the official guardians of spiritual values have allowed them to decay, and this because of their own neglect and not under any external pressure." She suggests that the triumph of fascism—whose essential creed is the worship of power—is the effect of a subservience of the intelligence, not its cause: "We see intelligence more and more enslaved by the power of arms and everyone today is compelled by suffering to be aware of that servitude; but even before there

*It was, I believe, Simone Weil's awareness of the moral failure behind France's defeat that made her react to it with such intense feelings of shame and anger and that made actual par-

ticipation in the Resistance (preferably in a capacity in which she would be in danger) of such enormous importance to her.

was any power to obey, the intelligence had already sunk into a servile condition." (64 OS)

Among the "official guardians of spiritual values" who had failed to fulfill their responsibilities to preserve those values she singled out writers for particular criticism. Weil was not, of course, arguing that writers should be moralistic (and she added that "the 'moral revival' which certain people wished to impose would be much worse than the condition it is meant to cure"); but the subject matter of writers is the human condition, and "nothing concerns human life so essentially, for every man at every moment, as good and evil." For writers to avoid discriminations of value—or, like the Surrealists, to set up the "total absence of value as their supreme value" (167 OS)—is to betray their calling and to become, of necessity, second-rate, to forfeit "all claim to excellence." Worse, because of their prestige and their influence, their general indifference to matters of good and evil is culpable: "I believe," she wrote in 1941, "in the responsibility of the writers of recent years for the disaster of our time. By that I don't mean only the defeat of France; the disaster of our time extends much further. It extends to the whole world, that is to say, to Europe, to America, and to the other continents in so far as Western influence has penetrated them." (166 OS)

Writers were not the only target of her criticism. She felt that science was equally and perhaps even more responsible for the enfeeblement of the sense of value that characterized the first half of the twentieth century. In the spring of 1941 she began to compose a number of essays—many left unfinished—on a variety of problems in the conceptions of Newtonian and twentieth-century physics, on how these conceptions affect the ways human beings think about the world, and on a possible way of knowing the world which does not exclude, in the interests of rigor and objectivity, the human mind's orientation toward value. These essays and fragments, which contain passages of extraordinary beauty, are very densely layered and very difficult. Weil not only assumes considerable familiarity on the part of the reader with the history of Greek and Western mathematics and physics but deals with such a multiplicity of ideas that it is not always easy for the reader to perceive the complex hierarchical relationship in which she has ordered them.

One of her major points in the long essay "Classical Science and After" is an argument against the assumption that the science that has developed in the West since the Renaissance is science in the only true sense of the word, compared with which all other systems of knowing the world are at best inadequate or at worst collections of superstitions. Any science, any system of knowing the world, she writes, is based on a relation of the human mind to the universe of which it is a part. There can be many such systems, of very unequal value; their value, in Weil's thinking, is not determined primarily by experimental verification—any number of different and even mutually contradictory systems can be experimentally verified—but on the relationship between the human mind and the representation of the world which they project. In other words, the human being, the human knower, is where science starts from, and the adequacy of a science is judged in terms of how well it connects the whole human being with the universe in which he lives. An adequate science, therefore, would include the aspirations of the human spirit toward the good and take into account the human need for beauty; it would thus be related, and not in opposition, to religion and art.

Classical science—the science that began in the Renaissance and lasted until the end of the nineteenth century—tried to see what happens in all physical transformations as analogous to work, to simple manual labor, and defined work, for its purposes, as the raising or lowering of a weight a given height. Its representation of the relationships constituting the world was thus based on what, in Weil's epistemology, was the way human beings learn of the reality of the external world, and it was this relatively close connection "between scientific thought and the rest of human thought" (30 OS) that in her opinion gave classical science its value. Yet, at the same time, she argued that the picture of the world projected by classical science was a partial one. It dealt with the abstraction of work but not with the worker; it left the human mind, and the aspirations toward the good which for her were virtually a definition of the mind, out of the picture.

Simone Weil accepted, as one of the givens of the human condition, the need of the mind for unity—for a unifying order within apparent diversity—and the initial frustration of that need in the mind's encounter with the multiplicity of the world. The mind is subject to the rending exigencies of time and space: "The thinking being is divided from himself, in his most animal desire and in his highest aspiration, by the distance in time between what he is and what he is tending to be.... and the extended world is made up of everything that escapes him, since he is confined to one point, like a chained prisoner, and cannot be anywhere else except at the price of time and effort and of abandoning the point he started from." (16 OS) Weil saw the anguish of this contradiction between the mind's needs and matter's necessities embodied in "an admirable image of the Manichaeans" which portrays the spirit as "rent and fragmented into pieces which are dispersed throughout space, throughout extended matter. It is crucified upon extension; and is not the cross the symbol of extension, being composed of two perpendicular directions which define it? The spirit is also crucified upon time, dispersed in fragments

throughout time, and it is the same ordeal by rending."
(16 OS) To counterbalance this "ordeal by rending" by
the creation or discovery of order within the material
world is, Weil felt, a profound human need; without the
possibility of at least symbolic mastery of time and space,
she believed, "man could not live."

     She saw in every form of genuine art a means of
this symbolic mastery; through suitable arrangements of
objects in space or the recurrence of sounds in time, art
"enables man to embrace in a single act of thought a
juxtaposition of places which is equivalent to all places,
a succession of instants equivalent to all instants." (17
OS) Science should also be, she felt, a study of the
conditions of order that can be discerned in the world, a
study that relates the objective world to the mind by
revealing in the world itself an order which indicates an
ordering Mind. Such, indeed, Weil felt, had been the
science of ancient Greece; the Greeks' "sole aim," she
wrote in a letter to her brother in 1940, "was to conceive
more and more clearly an identity of structure between
the human mind and the universe." (117 L) Their science
was a rigorous study of the necessities governing the
material world and at the same time a pursuit of the
knowledge of God by means of what she called the "imitation"—the reconstruction in one's own mind—of God's
thought inscribed in the universe: "the imitation of God
was assisted by the study of mathematics, in so far as
one conceived the universe to be subject to mathematical
laws, which made the geometer an imitator of the supreme lawgiver." (117–8 L) For the Greeks, science,
art, and religion were different aspects of the same need
of the human mind for unity; and they found, in and
underlying the diversity of the world, signs of order, of
unity, that made it possible for them to love the world
and see it not as a place of exile but as a home. Both
their art and their science revealed, Weil writes, a "kin-

ship between the human mind and the universe, so that the world is seen as 'the city of all rational beings.'" (118 L)

Both the conception of man in Greek science and the conclusions about his relation to the world are very different from their counterparts in post-Renaissance science; the latter is without relation to art or religion and is oriented toward the mastery of nature. We see the world as "blind necessity which constrains us," Weil writes, and it "appears to us as a thing to overcome." (21 OS) To the Greeks, by contrast, that same necessity, which is revealed in geometry, "was a thing to love, because it is God himself who is the perpetual geometer."

Weil's point is clear. Philosophical assumptions about the nature of man and the possible interpretations of the world precede and shape the development of a science, and the picture of the world elaborated by a science affects the way we regard the world and conceive our relation to it. It is for this reason that she was so gravely concerned about the loss of the analogy between the laws of nature and the conditions of work that accompanied the emergence of modern science at the beginning of the twentieth century. In leaving behind the work analogy, in speaking of time as a fourth dimension and space as curved,* modern science was abandoning a model of the world that was similar to the one that all human beings experience and was offering instead something entirely foreign to human sense experience. Such a model could not fail, she thought, to undermine the idea that there was an "identity of structure between the human mind and the universe" and that the universe was intelligible

---

*Weil did not reject the mathematics behind these conceptions, but she continually questioned the necessity of deriving from mathematics conceptions totally foreign to human sense experience.

to the reason "common to all." The model of the relationship of the mind to the world implicit in the then-dominant interpretation of modern science was, she argued, virtually barren of human meaning; it consisted only in a relationship between algebraic thinking and technological applications.

Simone Weil discussed a number of the consequences attendant on the development of modern science, but she thought that none was more serious than what she called the loss of the idea of truth. "The idea of truth," she pointed out "had been very closely associated with science in the eighteenth century, and especially in the nineteenth" (even though, she added dryly, "the association was very erroneous"). However, because science and truth were linked in the popular mind, "the disappearance of scientific truth amounts, in our eyes, to the disappearance of truth itself, accustomed as we are to take one for the other." (207 SS; cf. 63 OS)

While granting that it is impossible for "men of flesh and blood in this world to have any representation of truth that is not defective," she argues that, nevertheless, "they must have one—an imperfect image of the non-representable truth which we once saw, as Plato says, beyond the sky." (62 OS) Without some representation of truth, the intelligence has nothing toward which to direct its efforts or to use as its guide; and when truth disappears, "utility at once takes its place, because man always directs his effort towards some good or other." The intelligence can judge utility only if it is judging it against some higher standard than usefulness. Without that higher standard,

utility becomes something which the intelligence is no longer entitled to define or to judge, but only to serve. From being the arbiter, intelligence becomes the servant, and gets its orders from the desires. And, further, public opinion then replaces conscience as sovereign mistress of thought, because man always submits his thought to some higher control, which is superior either in value or else in power. This is where we are today. Everything is oriented toward utility, which nobody thinks of defining; public opinion reigns supreme, in the village of scientists as in the great nations. It is as though we had returned to the age of Protagoras and the Sophists, the age when the art of persuasion—whose modern equivalent is advertising slogans, publicity, propaganda meetings, the press, the cinema, and radio—took the place of thought and controlled the fate of cities and accomplished coups d'etat. . . . Only today it is not the fate of Greece but of the entire world that is at stake. (64 OS)

Weil was talking about Europe in 1941, but her description of the cultural consequences of the loss of the idea of truth is as valid today as it was forty years ago.

7

1941–1942

The early pages of Simone Weil's Marseilles *Notebooks* reflect an oblique but obsessive concern with the moral problems of war and the relationship between contemplation of God on the one hand and action (especially action in war) on the other. She had read the *Bhagavad-Gita* in Paris in the spring of 1940 and saw in the conflict of its hero, Arjuna, a mirror of the dilemma of those torn between a moral obligation to fight and a feeling of compassion for those who will be killed. In Marseilles in the autumn of 1940 she reread the Gita and studied other Hindu scriptures—the Upanishads, the Mahabharata, the Mimansa of Jaimina—and began to teach herself Sanskrit in order to read the texts in the original. She reflected deeply on the concept of God's nonactive action which is reflected both in the Gita and in Taoist texts. What Weil drew from these texts helped to form the understanding of the nature of God and his action (or nonaction) in the world that became the basis of the mystical theology she developed in 1941–42. In particular, the Hindu and Taoist conceptions of God's relationship to the world provided her with an alternative to the common Judaeo-

Christian conception which makes God a partisan in war. There is a "fundamental difference," she writes, "between the spirit of the *Bhagavad-Gita* and that of the story of Joan of Arc. . . . he makes war although inspired by God, she makes war because inspired by God." (25 N)

Weil had previously, in her essay on the *Iliad*, emphasized the similarity between what she called the Greek spirit and the spirit of the Gospels. When, in the winter of 1940–41, she read two articles by Déodat Roché on Catharism (a form of Christian gnosticism that was widespread in the region known as Occitania in the eleventh and twelfth centuries), she found a validation of her belief that Christianity issued from the same "stream of thought" that was to be found in Pythagoreanism,* the works of Plato, and "the mysteries and the initiatory sects of Egypt, Thrace, Greece, and Persia." (130 L) "Your studies," she wrote to Roché, "have confirmed a thought of mine which I already had before reading them. It is that Catharism was the last living expression in Europe of pre-Roman antiquity. . . . that Catharism may be regarded as a Christian Pythagoreanism or Platonism." (130–31 L)

Weil's enthusiasm for Catharism and, by extension, gnosticism and Manichaeanism has led some critics to associate her religious thought with the most extreme

---

*The Pythagoreans were a religious and philosophical brotherhood founded by Pythagoras around 530 B.C. Both mystical and scientific, the Pythagoreans were concerned with the purification and salvation of the soul, not so much by religious (ritual) means as by the exercise of thought and the study of the mathematical relations in the world. The order of the cosmos being, in Pythagorean thinking, divine and eternal, by the study of that order one could reproduce it in one's own soul and thus be assimilated to the divine. Plato adopted the main tenets of Pythagorean thought; the Pythagorean influence is particularly evident in his *Timaeus*.

forms of gnosticism,* which include a complete rejection of the material world as evil and, consequently, a refusal to accept the Christian dogma that Christ was both fully human and fully divine. Despite Weil's personal asceticism, which is sometimes interpreted as evidence of her rejection of the material world, her ultimate attitude toward the universe is not one of rejection but of profound and all-embracing love; and in her religious thought, as will be seen, the Incarnation—a mediation between man and God that participates in both the human and the divine natures—is of absolutely central importance.

*Gnosticism is a complex phenomenon, and Weil selected from it only certain elements. If one accepts Hans Jonas's description of gnosticism (see *The Gnostic Religion*, Boston: The Beacon Press, 1963), one finds that there is only one specifically gnostic concept that has an exact and unqualified parallel in Weil's thinking: the idea that there is a divine spark, a purely spiritual element, in man and that it is distinct from the soul, which belongs to the realm of nature (Weil calls this spiritual element the "supernatural part of the soul"). Otherwise, similarities between her theology and gnosticism are only partial. Although both emphasize the transcendence of God and his absence from the world, for the gnostic this absence is total, whereas for Weil it is only apparent; in her thinking, God acts in the world, but "in secret," under the form of "something infinitely small," as is suggested in the parables of the leaven and the mustard seed. Her awareness of the profound disjunction between the deepest human aspirations for the good and the world's inability to satisfy those aspirations has only a partial parallel in the gnostic sense of alienation from a cosmos ruled by demonic powers; moreover, Weil's awareness of the contradictions of the human condition never leads her to anything like the total world rejection of gnosticism, in which the cosmos is, according to Jonas, "an object of hate, contempt, and fear." (*The Gnostic Religion*, p. 253.)

* * *

Despite (or even perhaps because of) the intense psychological stress of the war, Simone Weil's headaches were less severe in 1940–41 than they had been in years immediately preceding, and she felt well enough to work. Debarred from teaching because of Vichy regulations that excluded Jews from the professions, she decided in the spring of 1941 to look for work as an agricultural laborer. A friend sent her to a Dominican priest named Father Joseph-Marie Perrin who was known to help Jews and other refugees, and he arranged for her to go to work in August on the farm of his friend Gustave Thibon in the Ardèche region of the Rhône valley. Meanwhile, the fortuitous contact with Father Perrin led Weil to speak to him of her religious concerns, and she was soon seeking him out as often as she could to pursue what he called her "great preoccupation . . . the religious question."[1] She later wrote that if it had not been for these conversations with Father Perrin, the possibility that she might enter the Catholic Church would never have occurred to her. She believed that her opinions concerning the implicit presence of Christ in the non-Christian religions and her rejection of the Old Testament conception of God "constituted an absolute obstacle," and she did "not imagine it possible that a priest could even dream of granting me baptism." Father Perrin, however, was deeply impressed by the way she spoke of Christ, and he thought that there was no insuperable obstacle to her entry into the Church. "The question of baptism came up very soon," he wrote in his remembrance, *Simone Weil as We Knew Her*. Once the question was raised, she felt obliged to examine the problem very carefully, to "face the whole question of the faith, dogma, and the sacraments . . . closely and at length with the fullest possible attention." (73 WG)

She met with Father Perrin frequently during June and July, and early in August she left Marseilles for Gustave Thibon's farm in Saint-Marcel d'Ardèche. Although Thibon, like Father Perrin, was to become an important friend, the first meeting between the two was not auspicious. Thibon's first sight of her at the train station at Avignon was a shock; he was appalled by the "way she was turned out and her unbelievable luggage."[2] She had none of the "elementary practices which enable a person to pass unnoticed," and she very disconcertingly said what she thought.

When Thibon brought her to his house, Weil insisted that it was too comfortable for her: "She refused the room I was offering her and wanted at all costs to sleep out of doors."[3] This being out of the question as far as he was concerned, she gave in; but the next day a compromise was reached, and she was installed, "not without a few complications for everybody," in "a little half-ruined house on the banks of the Rhône" that belonged to Thibon's in-laws. Thibon was reconciled to the move after a while, but at the time he regarded the episode as an annoyance.

During their first conservations together he found his guest's opinions not to his liking and her intellectual aggressiveness trying. "On the concrete plane we disagreed on practically everything. She went on arguing ad infinitum in an exorably monotonous voice, and I emerged from these endless discussions literally worn out."[4] He was fond of Victor Hugo, whom she regarded as a "sonorous imbecile,"[5] and he admired Nietzsche, whom she loathed. She had little esteem for Pascal and none at all for Bossuet, both of whom Thibon placed among the greatest of French writers; on the other hand, she displayed what he considered to be an utterly extravagant regard for François Villon. But if she was stubborn and opinionated, he granted that she did not take offense: "The most blunt contradictions or the refusal no less blunt to continue a discussion—two things of which I made a habit with her—did not meet with those expressions of wounded self-love which in the intellectual world are still more frequent than expressions of intelligence itself. I always found her unshakable...I never found her touchy."[6]

He also found that she improved on acquaintance. Gradually, he became aware of the "beauty of her soul,"[7] and a deep friendship grew between them. They talked interminably—even if they disagreed on many things, they had a common interest in religion and philosophy (Thibon was at that time in the early stages of a writing career on these and other subjects), and soon he became aware of depths in her that impressed him considerably. "She was just then," he wrote, "beginning to open with all her soul to Christianity; a limpid mysticism emanated from her; in no other human being have I ever come across such familiarity with religious mysteries; never have I felt the word *supernatural* to be more charged with reality than when in contact with her."[8]

Weil's days at Saint-Marcel had a pastoral quality. She loved the simplicity of her life in the little house by the Rhône: "I go to fetch the water from the spring, the firewood in the pine woods, I eat vegetables just taken from the earth and cooked on a wood fire; and I continually see the light of the sun shine in a different way on the valley and the hills; and then, at night, immense stretches of starry sky."[9] In this close contact with nature she felt enveloped "with beauty, light, and joy." Thibon gave her the writings of St. John of the Cross in Spanish, and she led him through Plato in Greek "with a thousand explanations." Every evening after work they would sit on the stone bench beside the fountain outside Thibon's house and talk. Often she read to him from Plato and sometimes from the Gospels, in Greek. On one occasion she "went through the Our Father word for word in Greek" with him, and they promised each other to learn it by heart.

Simone Weil's parents, during this period, were attempting to obtain the necessary papers that would allow themselves and her to leave France for the United States, where their son André had recently emigrated. After she had been at Saint-Marcel for a few weeks, she wrote to them that if their attempts to get visas were unsuccessful, they might consider settling in the countryside near her, where they would be able to find a small but adequate livelihood. "We could cultivate some vegetables on a piece of land, with Thibon's help and advice," she wrote to them. "I could work now and then for the neighbors, and perhaps I could also use my pedagogic abilities in exchange for gifts in kind." She also thought that her father, forbidden by Vichy regulations to practice medicine, would "very often have a chance to give his advice . . . and no doubt gifts in kind would flow in."[10]

The Weils were spending August and September in Poët, a village in the French Alps, and came down to Saint-Marcel to visit their daughter early in September. When they returned to Poët around September 10, she went with them and spent ten days there, helping the villagers with the potato harvest. While she was at Poët, she remembered her promise to learn the Our Father by heart: "I said to myself that since I had promised to do this thing and it was good, I ought to do it. I did it." In the process of bringing all her attention to the task of learning the prayer, she found herself transported. In the "Spiritual Autobiography" she later wrote for Father Perrin she recounted the effects the subsequent daily recitation of the prayer had upon her:

The effect of this practice is extraordinary and surprises me every time, for although I experience it each day it surpasses my expectation each time.

Sometimes the very first words tear my thought from my body and transport my thought to a place outside space where there is neither perspective nor point of view. Space opens up. The infinity of ordinary space is replaced by an infinity to the second or sometimes the third power. At the same time this infinity of infinity is filled in every part with silence, a silence which is not an absence of sound but which is the object of a positive sensation, more positive than that of sound. Noises, if there are any, only reach me after having crossed this silence.

Sometimes also, during this recitation or at other moments, Christ is present in person, but with a presence infinitely more real, more poignant, more clear and more full of love than that first time when he took possession of me. (AD 24; cf. WG 71–2)

Simone Weil's immersion in the Our Father probably began about September 15. She returned to Saint-Marcel about September 20 and began work on the grape harvest at Saint-Julien-de-Peyrolas, in the Gard region, on September 22. Although the work was exhaustingly hard for her, she did not fall behind the other workers. "Sometimes I am crushed by fatigue," she wrote of her experience, "but I find in it a kind of purification. Right at the very bottom of my exhaustion I encounter joys that nothing else could give me...."[11]

When the grape harvest was over she went back to the Thibons', expecting to go very shortly to Saint-Remy-de-Provence to work for several months for a truck gardener who had previously agreed to hire her. The truck gardener, however, changed his mind, deciding to take on only locals so that he would not have to board them. At about the same time, Thibon recalls, Weil's parents "called her back to Marseilles where her presence was necessary for obtaining some visa or other."[12] She went, though she was now very divided about the prospect of leaving France. She spent the next six months, while the possibility of obtaining visas looked alternately promising and disappointing, in a state of extreme uncertainty as to what she should do.

* * *

From the time she returned to Marseilles in November 1941 until her departure for the United States in May 1942 Simone Weil was phenomenally productive. She filled the last seven of the eleven exercise books that

were later published as her *Cahiers* (3 vols., 1952–55;
English title, *Notebooks*, 2 vols., 1956); she wrote the
essays and letters addressed to Father Perrin and published in *Attente de Dieu* (1950; English title, *Waiting
for God*, 1951); she composed the commentaries on Plato
and on other Greek texts which she read to a small group
that gathered for meetings at Father Perrin's Dominican
convent[13]; and she wrote much of the material that appears
in *Pensées sans ordre concernant l'amour de Dieu* (published in 1962),[14] as well as essays on work, on morality
in literature, and on the twelfth-century Occitanian civilization that flourished in what is now southeastern
France.[15]

The bulk of this material deals with Weil's religious
intuitions and reflects her discovery of corresponding intuitions in the mystical literatures of various traditions
and, especially, in early Greek mathematics. These intuitions, in combination with her life-long concern with
suffering, became the core of an emerging mystical theology. That theology has a three-dimensional quality
which it is impossible to reproduce in a linear way but
which, when grasped in its totality, forms a coherent
whole.

Almost all of Weil's writing in this period forms,
in effect, a "composition on several planes" that reflects
the multileveled complexity of thought itself. The highest
thought, she believed, involved a simultaneous grasp of
ideas belonging to various levels,[16] a grasp that creates
a unified construct out of different aspects of, or per-
spectives on, the same idea. (Weil frequently used the
perception of a cube as an analogy of the way the mind
apprehends a whole which is transcendent to all of the
perceived parts. Though we possess the idea of a cube,
we never actually see the cube itself, only a variety of
surfaces that do not appear square and angles that do not
appear to be right angles.)

Weil's way of building toward a multidimensional understanding of a complex idea is most clearly evident in her *Notebooks*, in which different understandings and different aspects of an idea are successively explored, each understanding modifying and acting in concert with the others. But the same complexity underlies all of her late writings, even if it is not so apparent in an individual essay. Consequently, to fully understand Weil's thought in this period accurately, it is necessary to immerse oneself in all of it and to hold as much of it as possible in one's mind at once in order that the depth of her thinking on the relation of the world to God may emerge. It goes without saying that this is no small job. However, to do anything less is to risk taking what is only a part for the whole, or to remain on a level on which her thought seems fragmented and contradictory.

The closest thing to a summary statement of the underlying assumptions and the direction of her late thought is to be found in a letter Weil wrote late in 1942:

I believe that one identical thought is to be found—expressed very precisely and with only very slight differences of modality—in the ancient mythologies; in the philosophies of Pherekydes, Thales, Anaximander, Heraclitus, Pythagoras, Plato, and the Greek Stoics; in Greek poetry of the great age; in universal folklore; in the Upanishads and the Bhagavad-Gita; in the Chinese Taoist writings and in certain currents of Buddhism; in what remains of the sacred writings of Egypt; in the dogmas of the Christian faith and in the writings of the greatest Christian mystics, especially St. John of the Cross; and in certain heresies, especially the Cathar and Manichaean tradition. I believe that this thought is the truth, and that it requires today a modern and Western form of expression. That is to say, it requires to be expressed through the only approximately good thing we can call our own, namely science. This is all the less difficult because it is itself the origin of science. There are a few texts which indicate with certainty that Greek geometry arose out of religious thought; and this thought appears

to resemble Christianity almost to the point of identity.
(156–60 L)

To state the problem from the opposite point of
view, Christianity was, Weil believed, universal—catholic—by right, by virtue of its relationship to this "one
identical thought," but was not universal in actual fact:

So many things are outside it . . . so many things that God loves,
otherwise they would not be in existence. All the immense
stretches of past centuries, except the last twenty; all the countries inhabited by the colored races; all the secular life in the
countries of the white race; in the history of these countries,
all the traditions accused of heresy, such as those of the Manichaeans and the Albigensians; all the things which have come
from the Renaissance, too often degraded but not completely
without value. (52–3 AD; cf. 75 WG)

Much of her late writing reflects her attempts to
understand and present Christianity as the specifically
Western form of a universal core of mystical truth and
to establish, within the West itself, a connection between
the Christian vision and all aspects of secular life, a
connection by means of which every human activity would
be transparent to religious meaning. For this to happen,
she believed, it was necessary first of all to reroot Christianity in the Greek thought in which Western culture
also had its roots in order that the deep rift between
religion and secular activity that characterizes the West
might be healed. Her commentaries on Greek texts ex-
ploring the similarities between Christian and pre-Christian Greek writings were intended to establish the basis
for such a rerooting. The last of these commentaries, a
long essay titled "The Pythagorean Doctrine," provides
what is probably the most compact summary of the intuitions of Christianity she found implicit in early Greek
thought.

Weil's interpretation of Pythagorean and Platonic
thought differs significantly from the rather widespread

belief that the Pythagorean and Platonic dualism of mind and matter implies a denigration of matter as inferior and leads to a "flight from the world" into a realm of pure spirit. Weil saw in Pythagorean thinking, and hence in Plato, a profound interest in images of mediation between the material world and the realm of the divine, images which imply the existence of a relationship between opposites, an ultimate bringing together into harmony of elements which, on a lower level, appear to be irreconcilable. Thus the Christian theology that she roots in Greek thought is not primarily a theology of gnosis, of intellectual illumination, one of the conditions of which is rejection of the material world; rather, her theology has at its center the image of mediation between spirit and matter, the most perfect expression of which, she thought, is the crucified Christ joining together the opposites of God and world.

The concept of mediation itself was extremely important to her; it was, she thought, the human mind's closest intuition of the nature of God. She found this fundamental aspect of the divine nature reflected in the structure of the universe and in the structure of human thought itself. What we perceive as relationships—and "there is never anything in human thought but relationships"—is a "degraded image" of the "divine operation of mediation." (197 IC) If one were in the place Plato calls "beyond the skies," one would see that "the universe is nothing but divine mediation. God is mediation, and all mediation is God." (196 IC)

In her view, the Christian doctrine of the Trinity—that God is a relationship of Father, Son, and Holy Spirit—perfectly expresses the idea of the mediatory nature of God. She saw anticipatory understandings of this primal divine relationship in Pythagorean thinking; the Pythagorean Philolaus defined harmony both as the "common thought of separate thinkers" and as that which "locks together" dissimilar principles. She found in the first for-

mula an admirable definition of the Trinity. "Separate
thinkers who think together: there is only one thing—
the Trinity—which realizes this formula in all rigor."
(127 IP; cf. 166 IC) In the notion of harmony as the
"key" which locks together dissimilar principles, she saw
a profound intuition of Christ's mediation between God
and matter. This mediatory role of Christ was even more
clearly prefigured, she thought, in the Pythagorean interest in proportions of all kinds, especially in the pro-
portional or geometric mean between incommensurable
quantities. Such a mean is not only, by definition, a
perfect harmony between dissimilar principles, but because it can only be expressed as an irrational square
root, it is, in a manner of speaking, transcendent: though
completely real and exact, it cannot be expressed in nu-
merical form. Like the Pythagoreans and Plato, Weil saw
in geometry and its "assimilation of numbers not naturally
similar" (161 IC) a "marvel" not of human but of divine
origin. Greek geometry, which she defined as being essentially the science of irrational square roots, was to her
the "most dazzling of all the prophecies which foretold
the Christ." (171 IC)

The two primal pairs of contraries in Pythagorean
thought—the one and the many, and the limiting principle and that which is unlimited—Weil also saw as intuitions of God as Trinity and God as Creator. She
identified the one and the many (or unity and plurality,
one and two) with the Father and the Son, from whom
proceeds the Holy Spirit. Limit and the unlimited are the
Pythagorean principles underlying the created universe;
Weil identified the limiting principle with God the Creator, who imposes limits on undifferentiated matter and
thus brings an ordered universe into being.

But there must be in God as Creator, she argues, a
harmony (comparable to the harmony in the Trinity) between the limiting principle and the unlimited, and here
she initially encountered a difficulty, because as she

understood the nature of God, "there cannot be any relationship in God whose terms are not Persons, just as
the bond which links them must be a Person"; and inert
matter,* which does not think, "cannot be a person."
(169 IC) She found this difficulty resolved through the
crucifixion, in which the incarnate God suffered death
and thus was reduced to the condition of matter: "There
is an intersection between a person and inert matter," she
writes, ". . . at the moment of death, when the circumstances preceding death have been brutal to the point of
making a thing of that person." The crucifixion, by joining Christ to matter, brings matter—which is at the far-
thest possible distance from God, as time is from
eternity—into the Trinity.

Both the creation and the crucifixion represented to
her the most extreme separation of God from God, a
separation that at once measures the distance between
matter and God and bridges that distance by means of
the divine Love, the Holy Spirit, that unites the Father
and the Son across all the vastness of time and space that
is between them. The very distance of the separation
between Father and Son is necessary to raise the love
that unites them to the maximum degree, that is, to perfection: "in order that it may be the greatest possible
love," she writes, "the distance must be the greatest pos-

---

*Weil does not always make a clear distinction between the
unlimited (*to apeiron*), which is formless matter (Plato calls it
the "matrix," the "receptacle"), and inert or nonliving matter,
which, though lifeless, is not formless. In this essay she is
interested in making a point of contact between Christ and *to
apeiron* and for that purpose identifies the *apeiron* with inert
matter. Later on in the essay and elsewhere she will remark
on the feminine symbolism of the *apeiron* and identify the
Virgin with it (see 179 IC, 139 FLN). She writes in her New
York Notebook that "God, the Virgin, and Christ in his humanity make a trinity which is the image of the other trinity."
(207 FLN)

sible distance." (428 N) At the same time, Christ's death—his intersection with matter—also makes possible the relationship between God and matter which is a condition of the creation. She thus postulates that the crucifixion, like the Logos of St. John the Evangelist, is a preexistent reality which also has a temporal expression. (She defends the validity of this assumption by citing the Biblical reference [Revelation 8, viii] to the "Lamb slain from the foundation of the world.")

Inseparable from the fact of creation are the necessities of time and space, and Weil's understanding of necessity plays an extremely important role in her religious thinking. Necessity has many contradictory faces. It presents itself to our sensibility as "brute constraint," as "the force which governs the world and makes every man obey, as a man armed with a lash is certain to make a slave obey." (182 IC) To the intelligence, however, necessity is a network of relationships, a "fabric of conditions knotted one with the others," which is the object of mathematics and other operations of thought analogous to mathematics. As an intelligible but intangible web of relationships that makes an ordered universe (*kosmos* = order) out of formless matter, necessity is the thought, the will, of God ("God causes the existence of necessity to be spread throughout space and time by the fact that he thinks it" [185 IC]). Finally, insofar as it is the thought of God, necessity can be said to be the Christ, the image of God.

The harmonization of these contradictory aspects of necessity is brought about by love, by the human being's consent to accept the existence of all that is, including evil (except "that portion of evil which we have the possibility, and the obligation, of preventing" [184 IC]). As a result of this acceptance, one comes to see necessity "from the other side," as God sees it, to know that all of time and space, all that we experience as finitude and subjection to necessity and separation from God, is part of the "supreme mediation...of the Holy Spirit uniting across an infinite distance the divine Father with the Son who is equally divine, but emptied of his divinity and nailed to a point in space and time." (166 IP; cf. 197 IC)

The process whereby consent to necessity comes about is complicated. It involves the human being on all levels—the intelligence, the supernatural part* of the soul, and the body. The intelligence—the faculty of perceiving relationships—and the practice of intellectual attention play an important part in the preparation that makes consent possible. When one grasps necessity as a network of pure and conditional relationships, one can regard it with detachment; one no longer stands in relation to necessity as slave to master but as one who contemplates to the object that is contemplated. "Necessity," she writes, "is an enemy for man as long as he thinks in the first person." (180 IC) What she called the "I," the "faculty of thinking in the first person," is not present in the operation of thinking of necessity as a network of conditions; the process of thinking, though it is the act of the individual person par excellence, is, strictly speaking, impersonal. Weil broadly defines thinking in the first person as seeing oneself as the center of the universe, the center of perspective in relation to which all other beings, things, and events have value according to their nearness to the "I." This is nothing else than the natural human condition. With rare exceptions, Weil writes, "everyone disposes of others as he disposes of inert things, either in fact, if he has the power, or in thought." (173 IC)

The renunciation of the power to think in the first

---

*In Weil's thinking the supernatural part of the soul is "infinitesimally small" and for the most part hidden from consciousness. The faculty of consent belongs to the supernatural part of the soul.

person is a condition of true justice, that is, supernatural justice, justice that respects the capacity for consent in each person, regardless of that person's weakness. The model of supernatural justice is taken from Weil's conception of God,* who, though by definition all-powerful, does not exert his power, who withdraws himself from creation in order that it may *be*, who leaves his imprint on it in the form of intelligible necessity which matter obeys, and who grants to humankind the autonomy of thinking beings with the choice of consenting to love him or not. Although apparently opposite, the consent to love God is the same thing as the consent to necessity of which we have been speaking, the consent to the existence of the created universe, even though, by its very nature, by the contradictions which are an inescapable part of creation, it is in conflict with our personal will and causes us suffering.

The soul's consent comes about through a love which is a response to the love of God indirectly perceived through the beauty of the universe. It is the beauty of the world, Weil writes in "The Pythagorean Doctrine," that "permits us to contemplate and love necessity." (190 IC) The fact that we experience the world† as beautiful is a mystery, given the fact that the material world "consists

---

*This refusal to exert all the power at his command is for Weil what distinguishes true from false conceptions of God: "The true God is the God we think of as all powerful, but as not exercising his power everywhere"; the religions that are true are those which have a "conception of this renunciation, this voluntary distance, this voluntary effacement of God, his apparent absence and his secret presence here below." (130–32 AD; cf. 144–46 WG)

†Properly speaking, Weil felt, "nothing short of the universe as a whole can with complete accuracy be called beautiful." (165 WG) Everything that is less than the universe as a whole is a "secondary" kind of beauty, which is, however, of "infinite value" because it is an opening to universal beauty.

only of inert matter, dumb and deaf." (191 IC) What impresses us as the beauty of the world is, strictly speaking, nothing more than the obedience of matter to necessity; moreover, "beauty touches us all the more poignantly where necessity appears in a most manifest manner, for example in the folds that gravity impresses upon the mountains or on the waves of the sea, and in the course of the stars." But insofar as necessity is the network of relationships that constitutes the order of the world, it is the intermediary between God and matter; and it embodies and makes visible the obedience of matter to God. The essence of beauty itself, Weil suggests, consists in the beholder's intuitive recognition that necessity, one of whose faces is brutal constraint, has for its other face obedience to God." (158 IP; cf. 191 IC)

Weil speaks of the beauty of the world as a "snare" laid by God to lead the soul to the place where this act of consent may be made. In the essay "God's Quest for Man" she takes the myth of Persephone as an image of God's dealings with the soul. In the Homeric hymn to Demeter on which Weil's essay is a commentary, Persephone is enticed by the beauty of the narcissus which "Earth...brought forth as a snare for the maiden"; (2 IC) she reaches out her hand to pick the flower, and at that moment the earth opens up and Hades (Aïdoneus, which means "the invisible" or "the eternal") seizes her and carries her off to the underworld. Prevailed upon by Demeter, Persephone's mourning mother, Hades allows the girl to return to earth, but first he gives her a pomegranate seed to eat "in secret"—a seed which, once eaten, will bind her to him forever. "The pomegranate seed," Weil writes, "is that consent the soul gives to God almost without knowing it, and without admitting it to itself." (3 IC)

The ravishing God of the Persephone myth seems to be very different from the Weilian God who withdraws in order to allow creatures to be, but Weil uses this apparently contradictory image to emphasize that God's love not only leads him to renounce his own power but is also actively directed toward human beings. Indeed, Weil suggests, without this active love that makes God search for man, human beings would not be able to move from the natural level to the supernatural: "The infinity of space and time separates us from God," she writes. "How are we to seek for him? Even if we were to walk for hundreds of years, we should do no more than go round and round the world. . . . We are incapable of progressing vertically." (133 WG) We are able to cross the universe to go to God only after God has first crossed the universe to come to us.

In the Persephone story Simone Weil saw an image of how the natural love of the beauty of the world can be an "opening to God" which allows the descent of supernatural love into the soul. Almost any natural love can serve this function, can be a bridge (*metaxú*) leading the soul to God. All of those things on this earth which are felt as precious—concern for justice, love, tradition, art, poetry, music, science, work, religious ceremonies—are capable, if understood correctly, of being openings to God.

Once the soul open to God has been seized by him and has given its consent, there begins a process that Simone Weil frequently refers to as an apprenticeship— an apprenticeship in perception whereby one learns to "read" in every event in the universe the obedience of matter to God: "For the one who has reached the end of his apprenticeship, there is no more difference between things, between events, than the difference felt by someone who knows how to read when he is faced with the same phrase reproduced several times, written in red or blue ink, printed in this, that, or the other kind of lettering. The one who does not know how to read sees only the differences. For the one who knows how to read, it is all equivalent, since the phrase is the same." (115 AD; cf. 131 WG)

The process of apprenticeship involves the body and the body's experience of necessity, which comes through suffering. The love of God—or the consent to necessity—is a reality, Weil insists, only when it involves the human being as a whole:

Through joy, the beauty of the world penetrates our soul. Through suffering it penetrates our body. We could no more become friends of God through joy alone than one becomes a ship's captain by studying books on navigation.... In order that our being should one day become wholly sensitive in every part to this obedience that is the substance of matter, in order that a new sense should be formed in us to enable us to hear the universe as the vibration of the word of God, the transforming power of suffering and of joy are equally indispensable. (132 WG)

There is a final aspect to Simone Weil's theology of mediation in which the human being who has consented to the love of God, who has undertaken his apprenticeship in learning to see the order of the world in the brutal face of necessity, himself becomes a mediator between God and the world, an *alter Christus*. Unconditional acceptance of necessity is tantamount to the acceptance of what Weil calls *malheur*—translated as affliction, misfortune, distress, disaster, woe—which she defines as "physical suffering carried to the extreme limit, without the slightest consolation... accompanied by utter and complete moral distress." (429 N)

In affliction, Weil felt, the essential quality of human existence—separation from God (to exist means to be separate, to stand apart)—is experienced to the greatest possible degree in its naked truth. Existence—creation—is by definition wretchedness, inasmuch as it is necessarily less than God, necessarily imperfect: "to have created man in a state of holiness," Weil writes, "would be equivalent to not creating him at all." (268 N) Our misery consists in the fact that we are not *sicut deus*, like God, a fact that is only brought home to us when we are "gnawed by necessity" (235 N); but since it is the truth of the human condition, it is a fact not only to be accepted but to be loved. "Our wretchedness is not something that we concoct. It is something truly real, that is why we must love it. All the rest is imaginary." (411 N)

When the truth of affliction is known and consented to, affliction becomes a means of redemption, a means of bringing together what by the very nature of creation is separate: God and the world. The redemption is thus the completion of creation, a completion in which humankind plays an essential role. It is brought about through what Weil calls de-creation, which is nothing else than the surrender of the illusory existence we know as "I," the willingness for it to be utterly destroyed so that the soul of the living creature may be inhabited by God. (Her concept of de-creation recalls St. Paul's words: "now not I live, but Christ lives in me.") When the de-created soul feels the weight of necessity pressing down upon it in the form of extreme affliction, it experiences brute necessity as the total absence of God, as evil*; like Christ, it cries out, "My God, why have you forsaken me?" But the extreme affliction it undergoes is redemptive, for though God is *felt* as absent, he is nevertheless present

---

*Weil speaks of evil both as a necessary consequence of creation ("The mere fact that there exist beings *other* than God implies the possibility of sin" [192 N]) and as a consequence of the desire of human beings to cling to, and try to increase, their partial and illusory existence: "The imaginary existence of thinking creatures who believe they exist is what rebounds in the form of evil." (218 FLN) While affirming that evil is essentially unreality (nonbeing), Weil does not dilute the horror of our experience of it: "We cannot contemplate without terror the extent of the evil which man can do and endure." (GG 127)

in the transparent soul, and the soul's experience of evil is the contact of God with evil, of Absolute Being with nonbeing. In this contact evil is transformed into suffering, and "the suffering is impregnated with love." (191 WG)

The soul's consent to de-creation also makes possible the contact of God with all of creation. Although God as Creator loves "finite things as such," (483 N) God as Spirit cannot love material creation except through the medium of an incarnate spirit whose bodily senses register the reality of the sensory world: "This world made up of sensations—colors, contacts, sounds, scents, flavours. . . . is saved, transfigured by a redemption when the soul that has espoused God feels the sensations." (383 N) It is thus God himself in the transparent soul who sees, touches, hears, tastes, and smells the material world and other beings ("If only I could manage to disappear," Weil writes, "there would take place a perfect love union between God and the earth that I tread, the sea that I hear. . . ." [403 N]). And this contact, this love union, between God and creation is dependent on us because it can be mediated only by us. It is "our vocation to be mediators," she writes, "mediators between God and reality whose very texture is made up of our sensations. . . . Christ has redeemed the world to the full extent to which such a thing can be done by a man, a single man, if he is the equal of God, and to that extent only; but the redemption is continued in the person of all those who, either before or after his birth, have imitated the Christ." (383 N)

8

1942–1943

Although she had agreed to accompany her parents to America, Simone Weil did not believe that they would be able to obtain visas and therefore did not expect that she would actually have to face the agonizing decision to leave France.[1] But early in the spring of 1941 the visas came through, and her parents were able to make arrangements for places on a boat quite quickly afterward. In mid-April Weil wrote to Father Perrin saying that the departure was arranged but she did not wish to leave, and that even at this late moment "I have not yet made my decision quite irrevocably." (59 WG) The last thing she wanted was to escape from danger and suffering, and she was afraid that "in spite of myself, and unwittingly, by going I shall be doing what I want above everything else not to do—that is to say running away." (60 WG) Up until now, conditions in the unoccupied south of France had been very quiet; if she were sure that things would shortly get worse, she thought that probably she would stay. She begged Father Perrin to tell her if he knew anything that "might throw any light on what is going to happen."

What finally tipped the balance of her decision to leave France was her hope to see her idea for a front-line nurses' corps implemented. She thought that there was a remote possibility that if she went to America, she would be able to bring her proposal to the attention of influential people in Washington and London; and because the idea for such a corps seemed to her "to have been sent me by God,"[2] she did not feel she should pass up even the "slightest opportunity" of making it a reality. "For this reason," she wrote later, "I have decided, not without pain and anguish, to leave."[3]

On May 14 the Weils sailed from Marseilles on a French ship bound for Casablanca, where they spent seventeen days waiting to board the Portuguese steamer that brought them to New York early in July. They moved into an apartment at 549 Riverside Drive, and Simone Weil set about trying to find supporters for her nurses' corps. She wrote Jacques Maritain, who had come to the United States in June 1940, hoping that through him she could reach President Roosevelt, and she sent an outline of her proposal to Admiral William Leahy,* who was head of Roosevelt's special staff. She also tried to interest the Free French Committee; she haunted the New York offices of the Free French Delegation, and she wrote to everyone she knew in London.

---

*She had written to Admiral Leahy the year before, when he was the American ambassador to Vichy France, about her concern over the treatment of aliens in French internment camps. She told him that "for very shame" she could "scarcely bear to think" about the terrible treatment to which the foreigners— most of whom were refugees from fascist countries who had fled to France before the war—in these camps were subjected. America was at that time sending supplies of food to Vichy France, and Weil asked Ambassador Leahy to make the continuation of American generosity conditional upon improvement of the treatment of aliens in France. See Pétrement, *Simone Weil: A Life*, p. 398.

While the war and her exile from France were her most painful concerns, Weil also tried while in New York to formulate clearly all of her opinions which constituted or might constitute a barrier to her entry into the Church. In an attempt to get an unequivocal answer as to exactly where she stood in relation to the Church—whether, given her belief in the presence of divine inspiration in the non-Christian religions, her condemnation of the massacres in the Old Testament, etc., it would be possible for a priest to baptise her without "committing sacrilege"[4]—she sought out several priests and a theologian at Fordham University. None of them, however, was willing to deal seriously with the issues she was raising. One priest, she reported, "told me that after I had expended sufficient effort in understanding them, I could certainly read the stories of the massacres in the Old Testament in the proper spirit, given the fact that he doesn't encounter any difficulty."[5] She finally wrote a very lengthy letter (which has been published as *Letter to a Priest*, 1954)[6] to Father R. P. Couturier, a Dominican who had been recommended to her by Jacques Maritain, but her questions remained unanswered.

As she had done in Marseilles, in New York Weil filled "notebook after notebook" with her thoughts. Much of her New York Notebook (published in *First and Last Notebooks*, 1970) deals with folklore, fairy tales, myths, and stories from various religious traditions. All of these stories, she felt, expressed in different ways the relationship of God to man; she especially saw in them images of God seeking man and intuitions of a profound truth about the nature of God, "that God is good before being powerful." (106 GTG) Both the stories of Prometheus and Krishna, for instance, as well as those of the life and death of Christ, reveal God sacrificing himself for men out of love. (cf. 122 GTG) Everything which reflected such an understanding of God was, she felt, Christian in essence, belonging to the Christian inspi-

ration even if it antedated historical Christianity: "everything which is true," she wrote in her New York Notebook,
"is Christian." (80 FLN) Christianity, understood in this
sense, could be truly catholic, truly universal, embracing
everything in all traditions which is a genuine manifestation of one transcendent and inexpressible truth.

In the face of the present moral and spiritual crisis,
she thought, it was of the utmost urgency for Christianity
to be "truly incarnated," for the "whole of life to become
permeated by the Christian inspiration." (109 GTG) This,
she insisted, could not happen as long as the present
"watertight division" between spiritual life and secular
life remained intact. But an end to that division was
possible, she believed, if it were understood that Greek
thought, in which Western secular civilization has its
roots, is related to a religious inspiration which, "although chronologically pre-Christian, was Christian in
essence." (109 GTG)

Parallel to her sense of the urgent need for spiritual
values to be infused into every sphere of secular life was
her awareness of the danger of religious totalitarianism.
"How can Christianity," she asks, "impregnate everything, without being totalitarian? All in all, and not totalitarian?" (117 FLN) The mysteries of the faith, she
recognized, "can be and have been used in the same way
as Lenin used the Marxian dialectic . . . : they are used,
by shrewd manipulation of the anathema,* for the total
enslavement of minds." (109 FLN) Inasmuch as the
Church had, in the Inquisition of the thirteenth century,
"set up a beginning of totalitarianism," Weil feared that
it was "not without a certain responsibility for the events
of the present day."

---

*She meant by this that the totalitarian parties control their
members through a mechanism analogous to the Church's formula of excommunication, *anathema sit* ("let him [who thinks
such and such] be accursed").

Both for the sake of the Church (so that it could fulfill its mission to be catholic in fact as well as in name) and for the sake of the world, Simone Weil felt that a "philosophical clean-up" (314 N) of Catholicism was necessary—a cleanup that would both repudiate the use of the anathema and clarify the Church's position on matters of doctrine about which she had been given, in her discussions with priests, "different, and often dubitative, answers." (124 GTG) This lack of clarity, she felt, created an "impossible situation" when at the same time the Church demands (in the catechism of the Council of Trent) adherence to all of its teaching. She meditated long and attentively on the problem and, a few months before her death, recommended—with what seems sublime arrogance but may equally well be sublime simplicity—a solution. Since in practice the Church "recognizes that the definitions of the Councils have their significance only relative to their historical context," she wrote, and since it is "impossible for the non-specialist to know this context, and often even for the specialist because of the lack of documents," it seemed to her to follow that "the proclamations of *anathema sit* are only history. They have no present value." This being the case, it would be sufficient for the Church "to put into words what is already more or less the practice, by proclaiming officially that adherence in one's heart to the mysteries of the Trinity, the Incarnation, Redemption, the Eucharist, and the revelatory character of the New Testament is the only condition of access to the sacraments." If this were done, she thought, "without the danger of the Church exercising tyranny over people's souls, the Christian faith could be placed in the centre of secular life and of each of the activities which it comprises, and could impregnate everything, absolutely everything, with its light." (74 GTG) And until such a proclamation had been made, she did not feel—however much she desired the sacraments—that she could ask for baptism.

* * *

Simone Weil was desperately unhappy in New York. Washington showed no interest in her nursing corps proposal, and she wanted at all costs to get to London and work for the Free French there. One of the people whom she knew in London was Maurice Schumann, a former schoolmate from the Lycée Henri IV, who was now on the Free French staff and whose job involved liaison work between the Gaullist movement in London and the illegal Resistance activities in France. She wrote him of her great distress at not being able to share in her country's suffering; she sent him a copy of her nurses' corps proposal and wrote also that if it was impossible to realize the nursing corps idea, she wanted to be sent back to France as an agent of the Free French in London. "I imagine you are in a position to help me," she concluded, "and I urgently beg for your support. I really believe I can be useful; and I appeal to you as a comrade to get me out of the too painful moral situation in which I find myself." (145 L)

Schumann was very sympathetic; he spoke of her to André Philip, Commissioner of the Interior and Labor for the Free French Committee, and showed him her outline for the corps of front-line nurses. Philip found the plan "impracticable," (157 L) but he thought she could be useful; when he came to New York in October, he interviewed Weil and agreed to arrange for her to come to London as a member of his staff.

Simone Weil's departure was set for November 10. Her parents wanted to go with her, but her great anxiety to get to London made her fear that their applications might compromise her own departure, and she made them promise not to begin their attempts to get the necessary permissions until after she had left. (Their later efforts to join her in London, and subsequently to travel to North Africa where they hoped she could join them, were all fruitless.) She sailed on schedule, but once in London she was unable to realize any of the plans that had made her so desperately want to get there. She was given a job as an editor in the Free French Ministry of the Interior and was told to read proposals from Resistance committees in France for the postwar reconstruction of the country.

In many respects this work should have been very congenial to her; she was given a good deal of freedom, and was asked not only to evaluate the reports of others but to draw up her own ideas on subjects of lifelong concern to her. However, writing and reflecting in England was not what Weil felt called upon to do. She had an urgent need—a need that she identified with a vocation—to be directly involved in the war. When she realized that she was unlikely to be able to convince the people in charge of the sabotage operations in France that she would be of use to them, she appealed again to Schumann to have her sent to France to work in an information-gathering capacity for him and André Philip, adding that once she was there, "it should be arranged for me to be in contact with the sabotage organizations, against the day when they may need to win some objective at the cost of a life." (177 L)

At the cost of a life. This, combined with a reference in the same letter to herself as a scapegoat and with other references in her *Notebooks* and her correspondence, strongly suggests that at the deepest level of her being Weil felt called to a sacrificial and redemptive death analogous to that of Christ. A few months earlier she had written to Joë Bousquet, a World War I veteran who had been paralyzed by a bullet in the spine: "Fortunate are those in whom the affliction which enters their flesh is the same one that afflicts the world itself in their time. They have the opportunity and the function of knowing the truth of the world's affliction and contemplating its reality. And that is the redemptive function itself. . . . But alas for those," she added, "who have this function and do not fulfill it." (137–38 L) Only in exposing herself

to the risk of death in war in the course of carrying out
orders (even if she had to beg for those orders in the first
place) did she feel she would be in a position to carry
out that function, which she believed was hers also.

War, she had written to Bousquet, "is the affliction
of the twentieth century," just as slavery had been the
affliction of the ancient world. Ever since childhood—
"since 1914," she wrote Schumann—she confessed that
war had always been in her thoughts. (171 L) Later in
the letter to Schumann she was quite explicit about the
exact meaning of her lifelong obsession with affliction
and war:

Leaving aside anything I may be allowed to do for the good
of other people, life for me means nothing, and never has meant
anything, really, except as a threshold to the revelation of
truth. . . .

I have the inner certainty that this truth, if it is ever granted
to me, will only be revealed when I myself am physically in
affliction, and in one of the extreme forms in which it exists
at present. (178 L)

Whether she expressed her urgent sense of vocation
in terms of a desire for a revelation of truth that can come
only through extreme suffering, or a desire to have her
flesh worn down by suffering and transformed by God
into food for others, it comes to the same thing; and the
idea that she might fail in what she felt called to do caused
her extreme anguish. "I am quite certain," she wrote
Schumann, "that if anyone believes, even mistakenly,
that he has received a command from God and fails to
perform it through lack of energy or faith or power of
persuasion, he is guilty of disobedience. That is my situation at the present moment. It is a situation in my eyes
infinitely worse than hell." (171 L) Later in the same
letter she reiterates the anxiety her impotence causes her:
"Even as a child and when I thought myself an atheist
and a materialist, I always had the fear of failing, not in

my life, but in my death. This fear has never ceased to grow more and more intense." (178 L)

If her request to be sent to France were refused, she feared that what little usefulness she had in her present position would evaporate. André Philip had taken her on because "he thought me capable of producing ideas which he could use," (177 L) and she felt that her ability to produce ideas would not last much longer—first because "the ever increasing pain of feeling that I am not in my right place will end in spite of myself, I fear, by crippling my thought," and second because in order to produce ideas she needed to be "in a place where ideas can germinate in a mind like mine: in contact with the object." Finally, she feared that she would be unable to work much longer because she was near the limit of her physical strength, and her fatigue was growing.

Despite Schumann's sympathetic regard for her, he was unable to get her sent to France in any capacity. All of her appeals were useless; she was told "again and again that . . . there was no possibility" of it.[7] Her disappointment was devastating. Nevertheless, for five months, until her health broke down completely and she had to be hospitalized, Weil fulfilled her responsibilities as an editor and generator of ideas for the Free French Committee. She worked long hours, often spending the night in her office and writing until she fell asleep at her desk. She wrote numerous essays and reports, some in response to projects undertaken by groups in France and others on the basic issues (the meaning of justice, the source of governmental legitimacy) which, she felt, had to be reflected on long and deeply before one could seriously plan a new social and political order.[8] Her essays cover the colonial problem ("East and West: Thoughts on the Colonial Problem," in *Selected Essays*); the war and the conditions leading up to it as an attempt to escape from the contradictions of good and evil ("A War of Religions," in *Selected Essays*); the shortcomings of the philosophy of Personalism and her answer to it ("Human Personality," in *Selected Essays*); and the philosophical inadequacies of Marxism ("Is There a Marxist Doctrine?" in *Oppression and Liberty*). She also wrote a short draft of a declaration setting forth her view of the human relation to the sacred and the social and political obligations deriving therefrom ("Draft for a Statement of Human Obligations," in *Selected Essays*) and a book-length text which began as an outgrowth of this essay and developed into an analysis of the effects, causes, and possible cures of the spiritual uprootedness that afflicts modern civilization. This text was published in 1949 as *L'Enracinement* (English title *The Need for Roots*, 1952).

* * *

"Resistance," Robert Paxton writes, "meant thought as well as action. Depression, fascism, and war—the second European fratricide in twenty-five years—all demanded an unsparing criticism of the European experience and hard thought about the new Europe that should be built after Hitler.... Because the totality of the crisis demanded profound change, they [the Resistance intellectuals] prepared nothing less than a transformation of European politics, society, and economy."[9] Simone Weil's contribution to the "hard thought about the new Europe" was not greatly appreciated by her colleagues in London at the time. Simone Pétrement quotes André Philip as saying, apparently in some exasperation, "Why doesn't she concentrate on something concrete, for instance, trade union problems, instead of remaining in generalities?"[10] General de Gaulle, having been shown one of her reports, is supposed to have exclaimed, "But she is mad!"[11]

Simone Weil, for her part, was sharply and impatiently critical of much of the work sent to London by the Resistance committees in France. Of one report she wrote, "They do not dare to state the problem clearly."[12] Of another, "These people are completely, exclusively, and consciously Fascists."[13] A draft for a new constitution drawn up by a group in France seemed to her even "less good than that of 1875." (92 EL) What was lacking, she thought, was precisely hard thought about root issues; what was needed was "*un effort d'invention*," a creative effort that could draw inspiration from its transcendent source.

The practice of attention directed beyond this world toward absolute good—the basic method of Weil's mystical theology—is also central to her late political thought. Her "Draft for a Statement of Human Obligations" sets forth her fundamental assumptions in summary form:

There is a reality outside the world, that is to say, outside space and time, outside man's mental universe, outside any sphere whatsoever that is accessible to human faculties. Corresponding to this reality, at the centre of the human heart, is the longing for an absolute good, a longing which is always there and is never appeased by any object in this world....

That reality is the unique source of all the good that can exist in this world: that is to say, all beauty, all truth, all justice, all legitimacy, all order, and all human behavior that is mindful of obligations.

Those minds whose attention and love are turned towards that reality are the sole intermediary through which good can descend from there and come among men.

Although it is beyond the reach of any human faculties, man has the power of turning his attention and love towards it. (220 SE)

If the reality outside this world is the sole source of justice, a politics that is concerned with justice and the public good—and not with power—must be oriented to that reality. The practice of politics, in other words, needs to be conceived as an art: "why should politics," Weil asks, "which decide the fate of peoples and whose object is justice, demand any less concentration than art and science, whose respective objects are beauty and truth?" (216 NR)

But if politics is conceived as an art, its practitioners need to be artists, that is, lovers of justice whose work is to embody in a material form—in this case, in the social order—the nonrepresentable ideal which serves them as a model. Ideally, she argues, political power should be exercised only by individuals whose attention is actually directed to the good beyond this world, because it is that orientation alone that makes possible the perception of the fundamental equality of all human beings. "It is impossible," Weil writes, "to feel equal respect for things that are in fact unequal unless respect is given to something that is identical in all of them. Men are unequal in all their relations with the things of this world, without exception. The only thing that is identical in all men is the presence of a link with the reality outside the world." (221 SE) But inasmuch as "real contact with this central and essential fact of human nature" is dependent on "really directing the attention beyond the world," only someone who has actually given his consent and love to the absolute good is able to regard all human beings as equal; only to such a person,* Weil writes, are all human beings real.

Orientation toward absolute good inevitably produces practical consequences. The person who recognizes that all human beings are worthy of respect naturally expresses that respect in concern for the satisfaction of their vital needs. Weil observes that people everywhere have recognized an obligation to satisfy basic human needs and have regarded progress "as being, in the first place, a transition to a state of human society in which people will not suffer from hunger." (6 NR) But the soul

---

*She did not mean, of course, only a professedly religious person. "Whatever formulation of belief or disbelief a man may choose to make, if his heart inclines him to feel [universal respect toward all human beings], then he in fact also recognizes a reality other than this world's reality." (220 SE)

also, she adds, has needs as real as those of the body, needs which, if they are not satisfied, reduce human beings to "a state more or less resembling death, more or less akin to a purely vegetative existence." (7 NR) It is of the first order of importance to discern and define these needs, to distinguish "between what is fundamental and what is fortuitous"; for without a clear understanding of what constitutes human needs, one is hardly able to design a political structure that, except randomly and haphazardly, can satisfy them.

Weil began by setting forth the needs of the soul in antithetical pairs which must "combine together to form a balance." (12 NR) In the first and relatively brief summary she sketched in the "Statement of Human Obligations," the opposing pair structure is quite explicit: the need for equality is set against the need for hierarchy; that of liberty against consented obedience; the need for truth (i.e., protection against error) against the need for freedom of opinion. When she elaborated on the needs of the soul more fully in *The Need for Roots*, she did not formally present them in terms of antithetical pairs, though she retained the idea that each need had its opposite.

What underlies the presentation of needs in terms of opposites is Weil's understanding of the importance of limit. The unchecked motion toward limitlessness, in her thinking, is always a motion away from the limiting principle, from God; the desire to escape from all limits in the name of freedom (which has played such a large part in twentieth-century thinking) was to her the sign of a profound intellectual and spiritual confusion, a grave mistake about the fundamental nature of things. She insisted that neither the body's nor the soul's real needs (as distinguished from "fancies or vices") are unlimited: "A miser never has enough gold, but the time comes when any man provided with an unlimited supply of bread finds he has had enough." Similarly, she emphasized the natural alternation between a need and its opposite: man "requires food, but also an interval between his meals; he requires warmth and coolness, rest and exercise." (12 NR)

The major part of *The Need for Roots* consists of an examination of what Weil calls the disease of uprootedness, which she considered "by far the most dangerous malady to which human societies are exposed," (45 NR) and with the need to be rooted, which she regarded as "perhaps the most important and least recognized need of the human soul." (43 NR) She describes at some length the contemporary manifestations of uprootedness. The focus of her attention is on uprootedness as it affects workers, both urban and rural, and it is evident that her lifelong concern for the formation of a "healthy working-class movement" (103 NR) is still very much in the foreground of her thinking. She also analyzes—largely but not entirely in relation to their effect on the working class—the consequences of the loss of what one might call traditional rooting mediums—small regional collectivities—and their replacement by "the nation, or, in other words, the State." (99 NR) Although she does not explicitly discuss the need for roots in terms of two alternating or opposed needs as she does with the other needs of the soul, there is clearly implicit within the need for roots a double movement consisting in the need to be physically rooted—in a place, a community, a tradition, an occupation—and the need to establish a connection with the transcendent realm. That connection, she believed, is for the most part made through one's physical roots, through contact with the storehouses of traditional wisdom and inspiration which are the heritage of a given culture's past. The loss of the past, thus, is the most serious of all the causes of uprootedness, for it is "equivalent to the loss of the supernatural." (207 SE)

"For several centuries now," she writes in *The Need for Roots*, "men of the white race have everywhere destroyed the past, stupidly, blindly, both at home and abroad." (51 NR) This spiritual deracination, combined with other uprooting factors—the breakdown of region-alism and the rise of the centralized state, the rise of industrialism and the shift of population away from the land and to the cities, the growth of a rootless proletariat, the importance given to money, the emergence of an elite culture that has no roots in popular traditions and is in-creasingly separated from its origins in antiquity—all this led to the condition of profound malaise from which Europe was suffering, a malaise which Weil saw ex-pressed both in the dispirited inertia of most of the dem-ocratic countries of Europe* and in the aggressiveness of Germany: "For people who are really uprooted there remain only two possible sorts of behavior: either to fall into a spiritual lethargy resembling death...or to hurl themselves into some form of activity necesarily designed to uproot, often by the most violent methods, those who are not yet uprooted, or only partly so. . . . The sudden collapse of France in June, 1940, which surprised every one all over the world, simply showed to what extent the country was uprooted." (47–8 NR)

Weil saw the task of the Free French as one of rerooting. The traditional forms of rootedness having been destroyed, the Free French, she argued, needed to learn how to discover "a method for breathing an inspiration into a people," (187 NR) how to facilitate a people's reconnection with the realm of value. The unhappy real-ities of defeat and occupation had brought about a new awareness of the importance of what had been lost, and in that painful awareness itself Weil saw the conditions in which real spiritual growth might again take place. It was in the very "depths of her misfortune" that France

---

*Simone Weil always makes an exception of England, whose determined refusal to quit turned the tide of Hitler's triumph in Europe. In England, she felt, living traditions from the past were stronger than they were in the rest of Europe.

might, Weil thought, be able to find "an inspiration in keeping with her genius and with the actual needs of mankind in distress."

In her late writings Simone Weil frequently personifies countries and speaks of them as each having a particular "genius," a "vocation" to be a recipient of supernatural inspiration. Inspiration, for her, meant the contact of a human soul with transcendent reality, the realm of truth, beauty, and justice, and the embodiment of that reality in some cultural form—in philosophy, science, art, literature, folk tales, religious symbols or ceremonies, political institutions. Accepting as a basic assumption the Platonic doctrine that "the imperfect cannot give rise to the perfect or the less good to the better," (44 SE) she postulated that all the arts of human culture had a supernatural inspiration. (342 FLN) She attributed the origin of language and the crafts to a revelation which is remembered in the myth of Prometheus bringing human beings fire and instructing them in the art of numbers and in all the trades. She also believed that each country of pre-Roman antiquity had "its revelation referring, not exclusively but mainly, to one aspect of supernatural truth:"

For Israel, it was the oneness of God, which became a fixed obsession. For Mesopotamia it is no longer possible to say what it was. For Persia, it was the opposition and struggle between good and evil. For India, the identification, through mystic union, of God and the soul when it has reached the stage of perfection. For China, it was God's specific mode of operation, the divine non-action which is plenitude of action, the divine absence which is plenitude of presence. For Egypt, it was charity to one's neighbour, expressed with a never-surpassed purity; above all, it was the immortal bliss of saved souls after a just life, and salvation by assimilation to a God who had lived, suffered, died a violent death, and became, in the other world, the judge and saviour of souls, Greece both received Egypt's message and had a revelation of her own: it was the revelation of human misery, of God's transcendence, of the infinite distance between God and man.... In the minds of the best of the Greeks there dwelt the idea of mediation between God and man, of mediation in the descending movement by which God seeks man. (45–6 SE)

The spiritual vocation of ancient Greece, she believed, found its perfection in Christianity, and the two together constituted "Europe's own vocation." This vocation, which involved seeing in every aspect of life a bridge between human beings and God, had begun to be realized, she thought, in the twelfth-century Romanesque civilization of the *langue d'oc*.* Christian but influenced by Pythagorean, Platonic, and gnostic traditions from the east, by chivalric traditions from the north, possibly by the remnants of the Druid culture of Gaul, the Occitanian civilization produced an environment in which "the highest human thought" (130 L) permeated the whole of society. Social life was characterized by a high regard given to the values of love, obedience, loyalty, honor, and purity. In the tradition of courtly love with its appeal for the beloved's consent, in Romanesque architecture with its concern for balance, in the concept of fealty in which obedience to a lord had its basis in an oath freely given and kept out of regard for one's own honor, in the Cathar religion with its extraordinary love of purity, in the lack of religious strife between local Catholics and Cathars— in all of this Simone Weil saw the budding of a civilization in which supernatural light indirectly illuminated all aspects of secular life, a civilization which, she argued, was the first fruit of the Christian revelation.† Although

*The region in which the language of Oc was spoken, i.e., the lands south of the Loire. It extended into what is now northeast Spain and northern Italy and was a considerably larger area than the present-day region called Languedoc.
†The Christianized Roman Empire was, in her opinion, Chris-

that civilization was dead,* its inspiration, she thought, could still be drawn on: "In the measure that we contemplate the beauty of that age with attention and love, in that same measure its inspiration will come to us." (54 SE)

The modern world, she argued, is desperately in need of such inspiration; in virtually every sphere it has cut·itself off from the transcendent realm. "Humanism was not wrong," she wrote in "The Romanesque Renaissance," "in thinking that truth, beauty, liberty, and equality are of infinite value, but in thinking that man can get them for himself without grace." (53 SE) Humanism looked for beauty and truth in the world alone in reaction against the "totalitarian spirituality" of the medieval Church, but the attempt to carry over the best of Greek culture while separating it from its supernatural orientation was like, Weil argued, transplanting a sun-loving plant into a dark cave. The plant continued to grow, but it did so in an aberrant way. The science that developed since the Renaissance, in confining its investigations to the material world in a way that excluded all

tian in name only. Moreover, she thought, in becoming the official religion of the empire, Christianity lost sight of the understanding of God revealed in the Gospels and substituted for it a conception of God modeled on the Roman Emperors. See *The Need for Roots*, pp. 271 ff.

*The Occitanian civilization was destroyed by the Albigensian Crusade, which was proclaimed by Pope Innocent III against the heretical Cathars (there were Cathars in all the cities of the Langue d'Oc, but they were most numerous in and around the city of Albi). The Crusade was launched by the French king in 1209 and continued for twenty years. The independent cities of Oc, which refused to hand their Cathar friends and neighbors over to the representatives of the Pope, were conquered and the region was brought under the French crown. The Cathar religion was eradicated by the Inquisition which followed the Crusade.

concern with questions of good, reproduced, as an image of reality, a world totally deprived of supernatural light. Because of the immense prestige of science—as far as science is concerned, Weil observed, "there are no such people nowadays as unbelievers" (239 NR)—this conception of the world as ruled by force alone has had an enormous effect on people's thoughts. Taken to its logical conclusion, it produces Hitler's view that the laws of force must govern human relationships as well as relationships in the physical world. Those who, without rejecting the materialistic world view of science, believe that "men can and should base their mutual relations upon justice, recognized as such through the application of reason," (241 NR) are caught in a "flagrant absurdity"; if everything in the universe is entirely subjected to the rule of force, it is "inconceivable . . . that Man should be able to escape the effects of this, seeing that he is made of flesh and blood and that his mind wanders here and there at the mercy of sensory impressions." (241 NR) The unacknowledged contradiction* between the world views of science and humanism has led, Weil argues, to philosophies such as utilitarianism, economic liberalism, and Marxism, all of which have in common the belief that matter, under certain conditions, becomes "an automatic producer of justice." (242 NR) This, she felt, is the confusion (which Plato describes in the *Republic*, Book VI) of the necessary with the good, the mistaken belief that the forces of the material world as such (in which Plato includes society), without the influence of the supernatural, are capable of producing what they are not; it is the belief that matter, in and of itself, can give rise to spirit.

*For Weil's distinction between legitimate contradictions (those which can be used as a lever to raise thought to higher levels) and illegitimate ones (incompatible ideas held as if they were compatible), see *Oppression and Liberty*, p. 173.

The recognition of the distance between the necessary and the good is of primary importance in understanding Simone Weil's religious and political thinking. "The distance separating the necessary and the good," she wrote in a fragmentary entry in her *Notebooks*, "...needs to be contemplated incessantly. It was the great discovery made by the Greeks." (363 N) In addition to the assumption that material forces can of themselves produce spirit, the confusion of the realm of the necessary with that of the good also leads to the belief that religious values can (or should be) imposed by force; it is the kind of thinking behind every form of religious totalitarianism and spiritual materialism. The nondivine origin of such movements is apparent, Weil insists, because divine influence in this world never involves force; it acts only in secret, in the form of something infinitely small (cf. the Gospel parables comparing the Kingdom of God to a mustard seed or to leaven). Weil frequently compares the good to supernatural light. It illuminates; like the sun, it is a condition of all earthly life, but it employs no force. Although she is concerned with establishing that there is a relationship between this world and the supernatural, that relationship cannot be truly understood, Weil insists, until the difference between the two spheres, and their different modes of operation, have been thoroughly recognized.

Materialistic science, Weil reiterates in *The Need for Roots*, does not recognize the legitimate place occupied by the good within the material world. First of all, it does not take into account the desire for the good in the human heart, which "is just as much of a reality as any other in this universe, neither more nor less of a reality than the trajectory of a planet." Second, matter and blind force are not and cannot be, she contends, the object of science; matter, qua matter, is unknowable. What the human mind knows are only the relationships constituting intelligible necessity; all we know of matter is that it is that which is subject to necessity. (cf. 179 IP, 261 NR) The object of scientific study is, strictly speaking, the relationships of necessity—relationships whose order and harmony cannot be the product of blind force but which reflect the obedience of matter to the ordering of the divine Intelligence. Thus science, she argues, is nothing other than the contemplation of necessity as the order of the world, an order that reflects— is the "radiant manifestation" of—a transcendent spiritual reality. Scientific investigation should be, therefore, "a form of religious contemplation," for the scientist's "true aim is the union of his own mind with the mysterious wisdom eternally inscribed in the universe." (262 NR)

In this understanding of science as the contemplation of the thoughts of divine Intelligence inscribed in the world, Simone Weil saw the solution to many of the intellectual and spiritual ills of the twentieth century. Such an understanding, by reconnecting post-Renaissance science with the religious dimension of the science of ancient Greece, would restore to Western thought its cut-off spiritual roots in Greek thought; it would end the division between religion and science, a division which distorted both; and it would provide an answer to the problem of the apparent sovereignty of force in the world. For, appearances notwithstanding, "Brute force is not sovereign in this world. It is by nature blind and indeterminate. What is sovereign in this world is determinateness, limit. Eternal Wisdom imprisons this universe in a network, a web of determinations. The universe accepts passively. The brute force of matter, which appears to us sovereign, is nothing else in reality but perfect obedience." (285 NR)

Citing Old Testament, Chinese, Hindu, Pythagorean, and Stoic texts, Weil argued that this conception was widespread throughout the ancient world: "The whole of humanity once lived inspired by the dazzling conception that the universe in which we find ourselves is nothing else than perfect obedience." (290 NR) Moreover, the thought "which really enraptured the ancients" was that the blind forces of matter were obedient not because they were compelled by another, stronger force but in response to love. She found evidence of this notion in several Greek texts. In the *Timaeus*, Plato writes that the divine Intelligence rules necessity by "a wise form of persuasion"; Weil identifies persuasion, which uses no force, with love, for in the *Symposium* Love is described as having nothing to do with force: "Love neither causes nor submits to injustice. . . . when suffering happens to him he does not suffer by force, for force cannot reach Love. And when he acts he does not proceed by force, for each one consents to obey Love in everything." (*Symposium* 196b, quoted 116 IC) Similarly, she saw the notion of obedience out of love reflected in the Stoic Cleanthes's "Hymn to Zeus," which describes the entire universe as being obedient to Zeus's "eternally living lightning"—lightning which Weil identified with the Holy Spirit, the fire of love descending from heaven to earth.

The idea that matter obeys eternal Wisdom because of love became for Weil a central conception in which all branches of human culture could be united. Such a conception would allow one, she writes, "to embrace, in a single act of the mind, science as an investigation of the beauty of the world, art as an imitation of the beauty of the world, justice as the equivalent of the beauty of the world among human interactions, and love directed toward God considered as the author of the beauty of the world." (159 EL) To make the unity of this conception complete, it is only necessary to add "work as physical contact, so to speak, with the beauty of the world through the pain of effort." With such a central concept it would be possible, Weil thought, to fulfill what she regarded as the particular mission of the modern age, the building of a civilization "founded upon the spiritual nature of work." (96 NR) Whereas in her early writing she had seen work as the way the human being comes to know the world, she now sees work as the most basic means by which human beings can consentingly participate in the loving obedience of matter to God which constitutes the beauty of the world. Physical labor is thus a spiritual discipline, the path to perfection par excellence, for just as the beauty of the world is "the radiance of [matter's] perfect Obedience," (300 NR) so human perfection consists in perfect obedience to God. Short of consent to suffer death itself, consent to the "daily death" of physical labor and to "the law that makes work indispensable for conserving life represents the most perfect act of obedience which it is given to Man to accomplish." (302 NR) The practice of physical labor, therefore, is an exercise superior to "all other human activities, command over men, technical planning, art, science, philosophy, and so on," in its spirital significance. "It is not difficult to define the place that physical labor should occupy in a well-ordered social life," she concludes. "It should be its spiritual core."

With these words *The Need for Roots* ends, unfinished. In mid-April 1943 Simone Weil failed to appear at work for two days. A friend went to her rented room on Portland Road in the Notting Hill section of London and found her collapsed on the floor. She was taken to Middlesex Hospital, where she was diagnosed as having tuberculosis in both lungs; the doctors, however, felt that with complete rest and hyperalimentation she had a good chance of recovery. They were perhaps not taking into account the degree to which her health had been undermined by years of overwork and inadequate nourishment; in any event, she ate very little, and her condition did not improve.

In July, thinking she might do better in country air, she asked her friends to inquire about having her admitted to a sanitarium. At about the same time her doctor informed her that he had decided to treat her by collapsing one lung in order to allow it complete rest; however, she refused the treatment on the grounds that the other lung was also tubercular. The doctor—who regarded her as a very difficult patient—thought it was useless to keep her in the hospital if she would not accept treatment and arranged for her to be transferred to the Grosvenor Sanitarium in Ashford, Kent. She arrived there on August 17, extremely weak, running a high temperature, and obviously gravely ill. A week later, on the afternoon of August 24, she fell into a coma, and died at about 10:30 that night. In the opinion of the doctor who performed an autopsy to determine cause of death, she died of "cardiac failure due to degeneration [of the heart muscle] through starvation, and not through pulmonary tuberculosis."[14] The coroner's verdict was suicide: "The deceased did kill and slay herself by refusing to eat whilst the balance of her mind was disturbed."[15] Her death was picked up by the local newspapers, which ran the story under such headlines as "French Professor Starves Herself to Death" and "Death from Starvation: French Professor's Curious Sacrifice."[16] Thus was launched one of the most dramatic elements of the Simone Weil legend: the "suicide," the "curious" (and, it is often added, futile) sacrifice made on behalf of the starving people in France.[17]

Despite the persistence of this legend, neither Weil's deepest convictions nor her behavior in the hospital fits with the idea that she willfully starved herself to death. "Suicide," she wrote in her *Notebooks*, "is ersatz decreation." Given the importance she attributed to the moment of death as the moment of the revelation of truth, and given her fear of "failing in my death," it is extremely unlikely that she would do anything to make her ultimate de-creation in any way "ersatz." Moreover, though she was convinced that "God will not bring me into [the truth] except... when I myself am physically in affliction,"

(178–79 L) she believed that real affliction is never voluntary: "If affliction meant simply pain and death it would have been easy for me, while I was in France, to fall into the enemy's hands. But affliction means first of all necessity." (179 L)

By the time she was hospitalized, her health was already ruined. Late in July she wrote, "What I am going to say now expresses an old (but increasingly strong . . .) thought and permanent conviction. . . . I am finished, broken, beyond all possibility of mending, and that independent of Koch's bacilli. The latter have only taken advantage of my lack of resistance and, of course, are busy demolishing it a little further." At best ("to speak like everyone else," she added in parenthesis, saying that for herself she accepted whatever might happen as "equally good"), she thought that her body might be "temporarily glued together in such a way as to be able to function for a few more years. A small number of years." But she thought that "even a temporary gluing-together could only be accomplished by my parents, not by anyone else."[18] (Her parents, of course, were unable to come to her, and she, to spare them the torment of futile anxiety, had concealed her illness and hospitalization from them.)

According to those attending her while she was hospitalized, Weil refused food by saying that she "couldn't eat when she thought of the French people starving in France." According to her mother, Weil had vowed on arriving in America not to eat more than the amount of food allowed by the ration in France. However, in terms of her actual behavior, it does not seem that her refusal of food in the hospital was entirely willful. She said that she "could not tolerate" certain foods, but she made efforts to eat. Moreover, she herself asked her friends to buy or prepare for her special foods "that perhaps she would be able to eat."[19] Finally, she seems to have managed to eat enough at least to keep going until the end of July, when she began to have what Simone Pétrement describes as "digestive attacks." After these attacks began, Pétrement reports, "she ate less and less and became even weaker than before."[20] It would appear, therefore, that when she said she could not eat, she meant just that: that she was incapable of eating more than very small amounts, probably as a result of years of frugal eating habits and of pushing herself beyond the limits of her energy. When the digestive attacks developed, the amount of food she was able to eat was reduced still further, to the point that, within about three weeks after their onset, her heart failed. But even in these last weeks—even on the day of her death—she managed to eat a little.[21]

Perhaps the suicide legend has been so persistent because it does, in an overdrawn way, caricature a truth about Weil's death; for it is true that she consumed herself. Her spiritual life, like the flame of a candle, burned at the expense of her body. The body's energy, she wrote in her London Notebook, was to be given to nourish the divine seed planted in the soul, even at the cost of the body's vitality: "when one is entirely deprived of this world's energy one dies. So long as my heart, my lungs, and my limbs can function at all this is experimental proof that there is still a drop of water to nourish the heavenly wheat. Make sure it gets the water, even if this means the death of the flesh from inanition." (349 FLN)

She was buried on August 30 in Ashford's New Cemetery, in the section reserved for Catholics.[22] A priest had been asked to attend the burial, but he missed his train and never arrived. Seven or eight of her friends gathered beside the grave. Maurice Schumann, who had brought a missal, knelt and read the prayers; Mme Closon, the wife of a member of the Free French Committee, made the responses. At the end of the brief ceremony Mrs. Francis, Weil's London landlady, threw into the grave a bouquet of red roses tied with France's tricolor

ribbon. For fifteen years, the grave remained unmarked.[23]
In 1958, it was marked by a partly polished square stone
of gray-flecked white granite inscribed:

SIMONE WEIL
3 février 1909
24 août 1943

Conclusion

Simone Weil was first introduced to American readers after the war, when Dwight Macdonald published translations of four of her essays and one letter in his leftist magazine *Politics* in 1945–47. Even though *Time* magazine (December 17, 1945) reprinted an eighteen-hundred-word excerpt from her essay on the *Iliad* shortly after its appearance in *Politics*, Weil remained relatively unknown to American readers until the publication of the English translation of *Attente de Dieu* (*Waiting for God*) in 1951. Between 1947 and 1950 three volumes of her writing had been published in France: *La Pesanteur et la grâce* (extracts from her Marseilles Notebooks, edited by Gustave Thibon); *Attente de Dieu* (letters and religious essays, edited by Father J.-M. Perrin); and *L'Enracinement*. Even before these volumes had been translated (1951–52), they aroused the interest of a number of American and British writers and critics who began to laud Weil as a religious writer. The editors of *Commentary*, who translated a five-thousand-word excerpt from *L'Enracinement* and published it in *Commentary* in July 1950, introduced Weil to their readers as "perhaps the most significant religious thinker to have been produced by France in the past two decades."

Six months later Leslie Fiedler, also writing in *Commentary*, underscored her importance as a religious writer and, even more, as a kind of religious figure. She was not, he wrote, primarily a social or political thinker but a woman whose passionate pursuit of the absolute made her both an unwittingly comic figure and a "saint of the absurd."[1] In effect, he transformed her into a literary character; he saw her as one of the "stock comic characters of the bourgeoisie: the female intellectual, the Jew who does not admit to being a Jew, the schoolteacher as small-town radical...the old maid."[2] He placed her in the company "of Don Quixote, of Melville's Pierre, of the tragic buffoons who can never keep our time because they are set by the eternal chronometer—of the Holy Fool, whose wisdom is an unforeseen power of what we call stupidity, the ridiculous raised to the level of the ultimate, divine, absurd."[3]

Whether she is seen as a literary figure, or as an archetypal Jew who, though "loathing her Jewish origins...was herself passing through the identical Jewish experience,"[4] or as a "fanatically dedicated participant in the most critical experiences of our time,"[5] a fascination with the extreme and dramatic aspects of her life has largely overshadowed serious and receptive interest in the whole of her life and thought. Susan Sontag accurately diagnosed the nature of much of the interest in Weil: "We read writers of such scathing originality"— Weil, Kierkegaard, Nietzsche, Dostoevsky, Kafka, Baudelaire, Rimbaud, Genet—"for their personal authority, for the example of their seriousness, for their manifest willingness to sacrifice themselves for their truths, and— only piecemeal—for their 'views.'"[6] This diagnosis is not far removed from Weil's own perception of the way she was regarded at the end of her life:

. . . you think that I have something to give. That is the wrong way to put it. But I too have a sort of growing inner certainty that there is within me a deposit of pure gold which must be handed on. Only I become more and more convinced, by experience and by observing my contemporaries, that there is no one to receive it.

It is indivisible, and whatever is added to it becomes part of it. And as it grows it becomes more compact. I cannot distribute it piecemeal.

To receive it calls for an effort. And effort is so fatiguing!

Some people feel in a confused way that there is something. But once they have made a few polite remarks about my intelligence, their conscience is clear. After which, they listen to me or read me with the same hurried attention which they give to everything, making up their minds definitely about each separate little hint of an idea as soon as it appears: "I agree with this," "I don't agree with that,". . . In the end they say: "Very interesting," and pass on to something else. They have avoided fatigue. (196–97 L)

As Elizabeth Hardwick noted in her review of *Simone Weil: A Life*, "Those who live with a breaking intensity and die young have a peculiar hold on the world's imagination."[7] For Hardwick, "dramatically reduced and vivid moments of [Weil's] thought and life" burn with the "clarity of the very reduction itself," and Weil's life seems "as if given in panels of stained glass." This is a beautiful image, and Hardwick creates a moving evocation of Weil; but more frequently the dramatic, the extreme, the seemingly even abnormal elements which are so often stressed in brief accounts of Weil's life produce images which, though arrestingly sharp, are severely and distortingly partial.

When bits and pieces are selected from the vast "composition on several planes" that constitutes Weil's life and work and are put together without deep reflection on the meaning to be found in them, the resulting picture has the one-dimensionality of caricature. The following is an early example from *Time* magazine:

By most standards, Simone Weil was an absurd and unattractive woman. Almost constantly ailing, painfully humorless and so intense she was either irritating or ridiculous, she agonized through a short life of 34 years and died in 1943 in a gesture that seemed to typify her gift for futile heroics. . . .

Her death left no particular gap—even among French intellectuals—because she had never seemed to belong anywhere. As a Jew she denounced everything Jewish; as a Christian she shrank from joining a Church; as a political worker she had no faith in politics; as a revolutionary fighter she deplored reliance on force. Yet today Simone Weil is looked upon by an increasing audience as one of the outstanding religious figures of her time.[8]

One-dimensional or exaggerated views of partial aspects of Weil's character and thought have continued to appear in reviews and articles on her even into the 1970s. It may be that, because she touches so painfully the deep and often unacknowledged ills of Western civilization, many intelligent and sensitive people, while recognizing in an almost visceral way the authenticity of her testimony to truth and the accuracy of her witness to her times, are obliged to take the edge off her vision and make it bearable by suggesting that much of what is admired in her "amounts to a frenetic displacement of womanhood"[9] or by viewing her half-mockingly as quixotic visionary, Clown, Outsider, Misfit. (Weil herself, in one of her last letters, compared herself to the fools in Shakespeare who "are the only people who tell the truth" and who are "listened to by nobody." (200–1 L)

That she has been seen for many years* primarily

*With the exception of the chapter on Weil in Roy Pierce's *Contemporary French Political Thought* (London and New York: Oxford University Press, 1966), there was virtually nothing published in America on her political writing until the

as a religious thinker has also had some unfortunate effects; it has resulted in the comparative neglect of her earlier political writings and of her lifelong concern with the value of work, with the working-class movement, and with the place manual work should occupy in a healthy society. Furthermore, to see her exclusively and in a narrow sense as a spiritual writer is to continue to think of spiritual and secular as isolated from one another and to inflict on her the kind of fragmentation she was arguing against all her life. As I have attempted to show, she is a writer with a profoundly holistic vision of man and his relationship to the world, one who has recognized and expressed as perhaps no one else in this century the ineluctability of human spiritual needs and the unsatisfied spiritual hungers that have driven twentieth-century men into totalitarianisms of left and right that are no less threatening to the future of civilization now than they were in the 1930s. To think of Weil as a "spiritual writer"—implying thereby the irrelevance of her thought to the problems of this world—is to fail to confront an idea implicit in her early writing and fully explicit and central in her last works: that man is both a political and a spiritual animal, and to neglect the spiritual side of human nature, and the obligations deriving therefrom, is a mistake with the most grievous social and political consequences.

late 1970s, at which point some serious studies of her social, philosophical, and political thought began to appear. See especially David Meakin's *Man and Work* (New York: Holmes & Meier, 1976); Hugh Price's introduction to Weil's *Lectures on Philosophy* (1978); and Conor Cruise O'Brien's "Patriotism and *The Need for Roots*: The Anti-Politics of Simone Weil" and Staughton Lynd's "Marxism, Leninism, and the Language of *Politics* Magazine: The First New Left . . . and the Third," both in *Simone Weil: Interpretations of a Life*, ed., George Abbott White (Amherst: University of Massachusetts Press, 1981).

Weil was, as George Lichtheim observed, "a moralist in the classic French tradition, the last of a great line which begins at the opening of the modern era and has ever since produced an unbroken succession of writers concerned with the whole duty of man toward eternity and his fellow beings."[10] *The whole duty of man towards eternity and his fellow beings*: the two are inseparable in Simone Weil, from the beginning of her life to the end.

Notes

Introduction:

Some Problems in Approaching Simone Weil

1. Jean Tortel quoted in Simone Pétrement, *La Vie de Simone Weil* (Paris: Fayard, 1973), II: 293–295.
2. Ibid., p. 295.
3. Jean Duperray, *"Quant Simone Weil passa chez nous,"* *Les Lettres Nouvelles, avril-mai* 1964, p. 93.
4. Hannah Arendt, *The Origins of Totalitarianism* (New York: Harcourt Brace Jovanovich, 1973), p. 62.
5. Simone Weil quoted in Pétrement, *Simone Weil: A Life* (New York: Pantheon Books, 1976), p. 392.
6. Simone Weil quoted in Pétrement, *Simone Weil: A Life*, p. 510.
7. Edward Grossman, review of *Simone Weil: A Life, Commentary,* June 1977, p. 81.
8. See Hannah Arendt, *The Human Condition* (Chicago: University of Chicago Press, 1958), p. 81.
9. Wilhelmina Van Ness, "What I Like," unpublished article in private circulation, p. 12.

Chapter 1:   1909–1930

1. Simone Pétrement, *Simone Weil: A Life* (New York: Pantheon Books, 1976), p. 19. Virtually all biographical information, except where otherwise noted, is taken from
   Pétrement's invaluable work.
2. Ibid., p. 6.
3. See, for instance, Pétrement's description (p. 11) of young
   André Weil using his elbow to turn a doorknob after he
   had washed his hands before a meal.
4. Dr. André Weil does not remember his sister as being
   sickly in childhood. (Conversation with Dr. André Weil,
   November 28, 1980.)
5. Pétrement, *Simone Weil: A Life*, p. 11.
6. Ibid., pp. 11–12.
7. Conversation with Dr. André Weil, November 28, 1980.
8. The Weils remained there until 1929, when they bought
   an apartment on the sixth and seventh floors in a new
   building at 3 rue Auguste-Comte, directly across the street
   from the greenhouses of the Luxembourg gardens. Simone
   Weil lived in the apartment on the rue Auguste-Comte
   during her École Normale years and in the years during
   the 1930s when she was on medical leave from teaching.
   The Weils returned to 3 rue Auguste-Comte after the war,
   and it is still the Paris home of Dr. André Weil.
9. Simone Pétrement, *La Vie de Simone* Weil, 2 vols. (Paris:
   Fayard, 1973), I: 33. The two-volume French edition of
   Pétrement's life of Simone Weil contains a considerable
   amount of material which is not found in the English translation.
10. Ibid., pp. 39, 53–54.
11. Ibid., pp. 40, 43, 50.
12. Interview with Sally Trench by Barry Farber, WOR-AM
    January 23, 1971.
13. Pétrement, *Simone Weil: A Life*, p. 43.
14. Ibid., p. 12.
15. Ibid., p. 20.
16. Conversation with Dr. André Weil, November 28, 1980.
17. Pétrement, *La Vie de Simone Weil*, I: 60.
18. Pétrement, *Simone Weil: A Life*, p. 25.
19. Ibid., p. 19.

20. Jules Lagneau, *Célèbres leçons et fragments, deuxième ed., revue et augmentée* (Paris: *Presses Universitaires de France*, 1964), p. 194.

21. Pétrement, *Simone Weil: A Life*, p. 32.

22. "Some Reflections on the Idea of Value," quoted in Pétrement, *Simone Weil: A Life*, p. 405.

23. Pétrement, *Simone Weil: A Life*, p. 46.

24. Pétrement, *La Vie de Simone Weil*, I: 110–111.

25. Pétrement, *Simone Weil: A Life*, p. 53.

26. Ibid., p. 63.

27. Ibid., p. 75.

Chapter 2:   1931–1933

1. See Pétrement, *Simone Weil: A Life*, pp. 76–77.

2. From an article by Simone Weil titled "*Réflexions concernant la crise économique*," quoted in Pétrement, *La Vie de Simone Weil*, I: 203. See also Pétrement, *Simone Weil: A Life*, p. 89.

3. Pétrement, *Simone Weil: A Life*, pp. 59, 73.

4. James D. Forman, *Socialism* (New York: Dell Publishing Co., 1976), p. 36.

5. Rudolph Rocker quoted in Noam Chomsky's introduction to Daniel Guérin's *Anarchism* (New York and London: Monthly Review Press, 1970), p. viii.

6. See James Joll, *The Anarchists* (London: Methuen and Co., 1979), p. 182.

7. From an article by Simone Weil titled "Trade Union Life: Notes on the Committee for Instruction," quoted in Pétrement, *Simone Weil: A Life*, p. 89.

8. Ibid., p. 88.

9. Ibid.

10. Pétrement, *Simone Weil: A Life*, p. 121.

11. From an article by Simone Weil titled "After a Visit to a Mine," quoted in Pétrement, *Simone Weil: A Life*, pp. 121–122.

12. Ibid., p. 122.

13. See *The Basic Writings of Trotsky*, ed., Irving Howe (New York: Random House, 1963), p. 244.

14. See "*Conditions d'une révolution Allemande*" in *Écrits historiques et politiques* (Paris: Gallimard, 1960), pp. 117–123.

15. These articles on Germany can be found in *Écrits historiques et politiques*, pp. 126–196.

16. "Prospects" is reprinted in *Oppression and Liberty* (Amherst: University of Massachusetts Press, 1973), pp. 1–24.

Chapter 3:   1933–1934

1. Pétrement, *Simone Weil: A Life*, p. 170.

2. From Anne Reynaud-Guérithault's introduction to *Lectures on Philosophy* (Cambridge: Cambridge University Press, 1978), p. 24.

3. Ibid.

Chapter 4:   1935–1936

1. Pétrement, *Simone Weil: A Life*, p. 224.

2. Along with some other workers, Simone Weil was laid off by Alsthom in April. After a week's unemployment she was hired at the Forges de Basse-Indre. She was there from April 11 to May 7 and was fired without being given any reason. She was unable to find another job for almost a month; during the last week of her unemployment she was reduced to living on three francs a day, which was not enough to buy adequate meals. She got a job at Renault on June 5 and remained there until mid-August.

3. "*Expérience de la vie d'usine*" in *La Condition ouvrière*, pp. 327–353; a translation entitled "Factory Work" appeared in *Politics* magazine in December 1946 and is reprinted in *The Simone Weil Reader*. Page references in the text are to *The Simone Weil Reader*.

4. From a letter quoted in Pétrement, *Simone Weil: A Life*, p. 248.

5. Jacques Cabaud, *Simone Weil: A Fellowship in Love* (New York: Channel Press, 1964), p. 129.

6. See William Shirer, *The Collapse of the Third Republic* (New York: Pocket Books, 1971), pp. 213–214; also Stanley G. Payne, *The Spanish Revolution* (New York: W. W. Norton & Co, Inc., 1970), p. 169.

7. Payne, *The Spanish Revolution*, p. 218.

8. Payne notes that in Catalonia this resulted "in a curious dualism between the de jure authority of the Generalitat and the de facto power of the CNT." p. 221.

9. See James Joll, *The Anarchists*, 2nd edition, (London: Methuen & Co., 1979), p. 208.

10. Ibid., p. 205.

11. See Pétrement, *Simone Weil: A Life*, pp. 270–271.

12. Ibid., p. 270.

13. This brief untranslated journal is reprinted in *Écrits historiques et politiques*, pp. 209–216.

14. Payne, *The Spanish Revolution*, p. 168. Early in the war many of the large estates and some medium-sized ones "were seized de facto by the UGT and the CNT (and in Lérida by the POUM syndicats). In many cases the soil was worked on much the same terms as before, save that ultimate control no longer rested in the hands of the landlord." Ibid., p. 238.

15. Pétrement, *Simone Weil: A Life*, p. 272.

16. Hugh Thomas, *The Spanish Civil War* (New York: Harper, 1961), p. 308.

17. From a letter quoted in Pétrement, *Simone Weil: A Life*, p. 296.

Chapter 5: 1937–1939

1. William James, *Varieties of Religious Experience* (New York: Collier Books, 1961), p. 305.

2. Gordon Rattray Taylor, *The Natural History of the Mind* (New York: Penguin Books, 1981), p. 108.

3. It should be noted that Simone Weil's descriptions of Christ first taking possession of her in 1938 were written in 1942. She seems to have been extremely cautious, initially, about giving a name to this loving presence.

Chapter 6:   1939–1941

1. Pétrement, *Simone Weil: A Life*, p. 355.
2. Ibid., p. 376.
3. See William Shirer, *The Collapse of the Third Republic* (New York: Pocket Books, 1971), pp. 609–620.
4. Ibid., pp. 699 ff.
5. Ibid., p. 700.
6. Pétrement, *Simone Weil: A Life*, p. 376.
7. Shirer, *The Collapse of the Third Republic*, pp. 715, 754.
8. Madeleine-Marie Fourcade, *Noah's Ark* (New York: E. P. Dutton & Co., Inc., 1974), p. 19.
9. Pétrement, *Simone Weil: A Life*, p. 378.
10. Ibid.
11. Ibid., p. 380.
12. Pétrement dates the essay on the *Iliad* after the outbreak of the war but before the fall of France. See p. 365.

Chapter 7:   1941–1942

1. G. Thibon and J.-M. Perrin, *Simone Weil as We Knew Her* (London: Routledge & Kegan Paul, 1953), p. 23.
2. Ibid., p. 116.
3. Ibid., pp. 116–117.
4. G. Thibon, introduction to *Gravity and Grace*, p. 4.
5. Thibon and Perrin, *Simone Weil as We Knew Her*, p. 122.
6. Ibid., p. 119–120.
7. Ibid., p. 116.
8. Thibon, introduction to *Gravity and Grace*, p. 5.

9. Letter quoted in Pétrement, *Simone Weil: A Life*, p. 428.
10. Ibid., p. 429.
11. Letter quoted in Pétrement, *Simone Weil: A Life*. pp. 441–442.
12. Thibon and Perrin, *Simone Weil as We Knew Her*, p. 129.
13. These commentaries, plus the long penultimate essay on the Pythagorean doctrine which Simone Weil completed after leaving Marseilles, were published in *Intuitions pré-chrétiennes* (1951); the bulk of this material, plus some other essays on Greek literature, was translated in 1957 and published under the title *Intimations of Christianity among the Ancient Greeks*.
14. Three of the essays in *Pensées sans ordre...* have been translated and can be found in *On Science, Necessity, and the Love of God* (London, New York, Toronto: Oxford University Press, 1968), and in *Gateway to God* (Glasgow: William Collins Sons & Co., 1974).
15. "Factory Work" (in *The Simone Weil Reader*, pps. 53–72); "Morality and Literature" (in *On Science, Necessity, and the Love of God*, pp. 160–165); and "The Romanesque Renaissance" (in *Selected Essays*, pp. 44–54).
16. Simone Weil's conception of the structure of consciousness has been borne out by recent neurophysiological research. Gordon Rattray Taylor writes that "the brain functions in a hierarchic manner. Just as vision is based on bringing together small fragments of information into wholes, and then [organizing] these units into larger systems, so thinking itself is structured in systems and sub-systems.... Furthermore... the brain's integrative activity functions over different spans of time, so that in this sense too there are several levels.... According to [Arthur] Blumenthal, it is the transformation of *sequences* of events into simultaneous perceptions that 'generate consciousness.'... To sum up, the brain is a mechanism which is constantly trying to extract patterns from the data it receives, and then patterns of patterns, until all is synthesised into the harmony of a single pattern." See *The Natural History of the Mind*, p. 318.

Chapter 8:   1942–1943

1. Letter to a Spanish peasant, quoted in Pétrement, *Simone Weil: A Life*, p. 467.
2. Letter to G. Thibon, quoted in Pétrement, *Simone Weil: A Life*, p. 480.
3. Ibid.
4. Letter to A. Weil, quoted in Pétrement, *Simone Weil: A Life*, p. 479.
5. Ibid.
6. *Letter to a Priest* is reprinted in *Gateway to God*, pp. 103–147.
7. Letter to Louis Closon, quoted in Pétrement, *Simone Weil: A Life*, p. 529.
8. These untranslated essays are collected in *Écrits de Londres* (Paris: Gallimard, 1957).
9. Robert O. Paxton, *Europe in the Twentieth Century* (New York: Harcourt Brace Jovanovich, 1975), p. 463.
10. Pétrement, *Simone Weil: A Life*, p. 503.
11. Ibid., p. 514.
12. Ibid., p. 508.
13. Ibid., p. 510.
14. Ibid., p. 536.
15. Ibid., p. 537.
16. Ibid.
17. According to the doctor's testimony, Simone Weil said she "couldn't eat when she thought of the French people starving in France." See Pétrement, p. 536.
18. Letter to L. Closon, quoted in Pétrement, p. 531.
19. Pétrement, p. 536.
20. Ibid., p. 532.
21. Ibid., p. 538.
22. Simone Weil never asked to be baptized. There is a rather unsatisfactory story—the person telling it declines to be identified—that, in the hospital in London, a friend took it upon herself to baptize Weil with tap water. See Pétrement, p. 524.
23. See Pétrement, p. 538; also Jacques Cabaud, *Simone Weil à New York et à Londres* (Paris: Plon, 1976), pp. 89, 92.

CONCLUSION

1. See Leslie Fiedler, "Simone Weil: Prophet Out of Israel. A Saint of the Absurd," *Commentary*, July 1951, pp. 36–46.
2. Ibid., p. 37.
3. Ibid., p. 39.
4. Arthur A. Cohen, ed., *Arguments and Doctrines: A Reader of Jewish Thinking in the Aftermath of the Holocaust* (New York: Harper & Row, 1970), p. 50.
5. Alfred Kazin, *The Inmost Leaf* (New York: Harcourt Brace & Co., 1955), p. 211.
6. Susan Sontag, *Against Interpretation and Other Essays* (New York: Farrar, Straus & Giroux, 1966), pp. 50–51.
7. Elizabeth Hardwick, review of Simone Pétrement's *Simone Weil: A Life*, *New York Times Book Review*, January 23, 1977, p. 1.
8. *Time*, January 15, 1951, p. 48.
9. Paul West, *The Wine of Absurdity* (University Park: Pennsylvania State University Press, 1966), p. 153.
10. George Lichtheim, *Collected Essays* (New York: The Viking Press, 1973), p. 467.

Bibliography

I.   SIMONE WEIL'S WRITINGS IN ENGLISH TRANSLATION

First and Last Notebooks (translated and with an introduction by Richard Rees). London, New York, Toronto: Oxford University Press, 1970.

Gateway to God (extracts from 1942–43 religious writings, edited by David Raper, with an introduction by Vernon Sproxton, and including an interview between Dr. André Weil and Malcolm Muggeridge). Glasgow: William Collins & Sons, 1974.

Gravity and Grace (extracts from the Marseilles Notebooks, edited and with an introduction by Gustave Thibon). New York: G. P. Putnam's Sons, 1952. Reprint: Octagon, 1979.

The Iliad, or The Poem of Force. Wallingford, Pennsylvania: Pendle Hill Pamphlets, 1956.

Intimations of Christianity among the Ancient Greeks. London: Routledge & Kegan Paul, 1957.

Letter to a Priest. New York: G. P. Putnam's Sons, 1954.

Lectures on Philosophy (with introductions by Peter Winch and Anne Reynaud-Guérithault). Cambridge: Cambridge University Press, 1978.

Bibliography   181

The Need for Roots (with an introduction by T. S. Eliot). New York: G. P. Putnam's Sons, 1952. Reprint: New York: Harper Torchbooks, 1971.

The Notebooks of Simone Weil (2 vols). London: Routledge & Kegan Paul, 1956.

On Science, Necessity, and the Love of God (essays collected, translated, and with an introduction by Richard Rees). London, New York, Toronto: Oxford University Press, 1968.

Oppression and Liberty. London: Routledge & Kegan Paul, 1958. Reprinted with an introduction by F. C. Ellert. Amherst: University of Massachusetts Press, 1973.

Selected Essays 1934–1943 (selected, translated, and with an introduction by Richard Rees). London, New York, Toronto: Oxford University Press, 1962.

Seventy Letters (translated, arranged, and with a foreword by Richard Rees). London, New York, Toronto: Oxford University Press, 1965.

The Simone Weil Reader (a large selection of extracts from a variety of Weil's works, edited and with an introduction by George A. Panichas). New York: David McKay Co., Inc. 1977.

Two Moral Essays ("Draft for a Statement of Human Obligations" and "Human Personality"). Wallingford, Pennsylvania: Pendle Hill Pamphlets, 1981.

Waiting for God (with an introduction by Leslie Fiedler). New York: G. P. Putnam's Sons, 1951. Reprint: New York: Harper Colophon Books, 1973.

II. Simone Weil's Writings in French

Attente de Dieu. Paris: La Colombe, 1950.
Cahiers (3 Vols.). Paris: Plon, 1951–56; new edition, revised and augmented, 1970.
La Condition ouvrière. Paris: Gallimard, 1951.
La Connaissance surnaturelle. Paris: Gallimard, 1950.
Écrits historiques et politiques. Paris: Gallimard, 1960.
Écrits de Londres et dernières lettres. Paris: Gallimard, 1957.
L'Enracinement. Paris: Gallimard, 1950.

Intuitions pré-chrétiennes. Paris: La Colombe, 1951.
Leçons de philosophie. Paris: Plon, 1959.
Lettre à un religieux. Paris: Gallimard, 1950.
Oppression et liberté. Paris: Gallimard, 1955.
Pensées sans ordre concernant l'amour de Dieu. Paris: Gallimard, 1962.
La Pesanteur et la grâce. Paris: Plon, 1947.
Poèmes suivis de Venise sauvée. Paris: Gallimard, 1968.
La Source Grecque. Paris, Gallimard, 1963.
Sur la science. Paris: Gallimard, 1966.

III. Books About Simone Weil

Anderson, David. *Simone Weil*. London: SCM Press, Ltd., 1971.

Cabaud, Jacques. *Simone Weil: A Fellowship in Love*. New York: Channel Press, 1964.

Gilbert Kahn, ed. *Simone Weil: Philosophe, historienne et mystique*. Paris: Aubier Montaigne, 1978.

Little, Janet Patricia. *Simone Weil: A Bibliography*. London: Grant and Cutler, 1973. Supplement, 1980.

Pétrement, Simone. *La Vie de Simone Weil*. 2 vols. Paris: Fayard, 1973.

————— . *Simone Weil: A Life*. New York: Pantheon Books, 1976.

Rees, Richard. *Simone Weil: A Sketch for a Portrait*. Carbondale: Southern Illinois University Press, 1966.

Thibon, G., and Perrin, J.-M. *Simone Weil as We Knew Her*. London: Routledge and Kegan Paul, 1953.

Tomlin, E. W. F. *Simone Weil*. Cambridge: Bowes & Bowes, Ltd, 1954.

White, George Abbot, ed. *Simone Weil: Interpretations of a Life*. Amherst: University of Massachusetts Press, 1981.

Index